Also by C. K. Williams

Lies *(1969)*
I Am the Bitter Name *(1971)*
With Ignorance *(1977)*
Sophocles' Women of Trachis (with Gregory Dickerson) *(1978)*
The Lark. The Thrush. The Starling.: Poems from Issa *(1983)*
Tar *(1983)*
Flesh and Blood *(1987)*
Poems 1963–1983 *(1989)*
A Dream of Mind *(1992)*
Selected Poems *(1994)*
The Vigil *(1997)*

THE BACCHAE

of Euripides

THE

BACCHAE

of Euripides

A NEW VERSION

by C. K. Williams

WITH AN INTRODUCTION

BY MARTHA NUSSBAUM

Farrar, Straus and Giroux

New York

Contents

Introduction

Euripides' *Bacchae* ends with a scene in which a mother reassembles
her son's severed bodily parts, parts that she herself has fatally
ripped. She puzzles over the proper location of each member, weep-
ing for the disunity that she herself has made. And the play itself
demands, it seems, just such an effort from its audience: an effort,
mixed with pity and grief, to compose and recompose the parts or
aspects of Dionysus, making of the hidings and revealings of this
strange god some whole coherent form. And it seems to demand,
as well, acknowledgment that this strangeness and disorder are also
in the spectators themselves, that they, or a part of them, have made
it.

But unlike the dead limbs of Pentheus, Dionysus will not be
set in any static ordering; nor will the recognitions that he, and this
play, offer to its spectators. Dispersed and yet himself, contradictory
and yet strangely constant, he resists human attempts to integrate
him and to pin him down. While the audience, like Agave, grieves,
trying to produce order, trying to understand, he smiles and moves
on. The goal of the confrontation must, then, be appropriate to its
object: not so much the resolution of his contradictions as a greater
awareness of their structure and of their relations—invasive, con-
soling, detached, transporting—to human life and its possibilities.

To begin this confrontation, then, we need to get a clearer sense
of the problems that face the interpreter of Dionysus, and of this

play. We begin to see them emerging if we examine the lyric sung
by the Chorus after Pentheus, deluded by the god and dressed in
women's clothing, has been led off to his doom:

> Oh, will I, some-
>   time, in the all-
>   night dances, dance
> again, bare-
>   foot, rapt,
>   again, in
> Bacchus, all
>   in Bacchus,
>   again?

> Will I
>   throw my bared
>   throat
> back, to the cool
>   night back, the
>   way,
> oh, in the green joys
>   of the meadow, the
>   way
> a fawn
>   frisks, leaps,
>   throws itself
> as it finds itself
>   safely past
>   the frightening
> hunters, past the
>   nets, the
>   houndsmen
> urging on
>   their straining
>   hounds, free

now, leaping, tasting
  free wind now,
    being wind
now as it leaps
  the plain, the
    stream
and river, out
  at last, out from
    the human,
free, back,
  into the
    green,
rich, dapple-
  shadowed tresses of the
    forest.

What is
  wisdom?
    What
the fairest
  gift the gods
    can offer
us
  below?
    What
is nobler
  than
    to hold
a dominating
  hand
    above
the bent
  head of
    the enemy?
The fair, the

noble, how
we
cherish, how
we welcome
them.

Hardly
stirring, hardly
seeming
to happen, it
happens sometimes
so
slowly, the power
of the gods, but
it does, then,
stir, does
come
to pass, and,
inexorably, comes
to punish
humans,
who honor first
self-pride, and
turn,
their judgment
torn, their reason
torn,
demented, from
the
holy.

The first step
of the gods, it
hardly, in
its great
time, seems

to stir, the
first step
  of the godly hunt
    of
the unholy, first
  step
    of the revenge
on those who
  put themselves
    beyond
and
  over
    law.

So little
  does
    it cost
to understand
  that *this*
    has power, whatever
is divine; so
  little
    cost
to comprehend
  that what has
    long
been lawful,
  over
    centuries,
comes forever
  out
    of Nature.

What is
  wisdom?
    What

the fairest
  gift the gods
    can offer
us
  below?
   What
is nobler
  than
   to hold
a dominating
  hand
   above
the bent
  head of
   the enemy?
The fair, the
  noble, how
   we
cherish, how
  we welcome
   them.   *(862–901)*

One of the most beautiful choral lyrics in all of Greek tragedy, this passage closes in a chilling refrain, twice repeated. And it contains, indissolubly, a mixture of beauty and horror. There is indeed beauty here, in the described content as in the describing language and its intricate delicate meter. The religion of Dionysus makes these women free to dance, to leap, to move with grace and power through the world of nature with the green joy of the body and its freedom. Their passage beyond civilization to a place empty of human beings is exuberant and joyful, an overcoming of constraints seen as inherent in the human world. On the other hand, the refrain suggests that they move beyond civilization in another way as well: in their thirst for blood, their pitiless belief that vengeance is the most beautiful thing. The imagery of the ode explores this doubleness. For as fawns they escape well-woven nets; but they delight, too, in hunting down their prey. (Dionysus has just announced that Pentheus has been trapped in his net [line 848].) They move with the light rapidity of the dance, but they delight in the slow, inexorable movement of divine vengeance. They flee constraints, and they gleefully invoke them against their enemy.

These ambiguities reach a climax in the refrain's final line, whose multiple meanings C. K. Williams has elegantly attempted to set out in this original and convincing version.[1] Literally, the Greek says: "Whatever is *kalon* is always *philon.*" *Kalon* is a word that signifies at once beauty and nobility. It can be either aesthetic or ethical and is usually both at once, showing how hard it is to distinguish these spheres in Greek thought. The *kalon* is, for example, the topic of Plato's *Symposium*, where it is a property of young bodies, of moral and civic institutions, of noble souls. Its contrary is *aischron*—"ugly," "shameful," "base." "Fine" is perhaps the best single-word translation. *Philon*, relative of the noun *philos*—"friend," "loved one"—means "beloved," "precious," "a friend to," "dear," "welcome." This ambiguous line, then, is the ancestor of "A thing of beauty is a joy forever." It expresses love for what is truly noble, truly fine. But what is the object of this moral/aesthetic appreciation? Vengeance and cruelty, punishment and death. It is not possible to separate the beautiful from the horrible. For the freedom to dance *is* also the hunting of the god's enemy. And the cruelty of the god's vengeance *is* a most beautiful thing, in the sense that it makes and has made possible the transcendent beauty of movement and passion that these women live, the poetic beauty by which the audience is moved. Dionysus, as he himself has just announced, is both "fiercest and most sweet" to human beings.

This mixture of fierceness and sweetness runs throughout the play. The story of Dionysus' arrival in Thebes begins with his birth from Semele, a birth that he himself describes in the play's opening

---

[1] For discussion of Williams's approach to translation of the choral lyrics (where his translations are slightly less literal than in the dialogue scenes), see pp. xlvi–xlvii.

lines. "Her midwife was the lightning bolt that killed her" (line 3: my own literal translation). A birth that brings death, a fertility that is blazing destruction: so this god's career begins. And since the lightning bolt represents in the story, as well, Zeus's impregnating penetration of his earthly bride, the event also combines ecstasy with fatality, erotic passion with the extinction of the self. The still-smoldering tomb is the setting for the play's action. The spectators watch it throughout, reminded by that monument of a contact between civilized human life and what is other than, outside of, civilization.[2]

Two groups of women worship Dionysus in this play. And both groups, in their speech and actions, display a mixed, a double, character. The Maenads on the mountain enjoy a transforming oneness with the fertility and energy of nature; they are also orderly and chaste. Yet in a moment they turn their energy to destruction, tearing animals apart, raiding villages, snatching children from their homes. The killing of Pentheus is no exception; it is part of a general pattern of frenzy, blindness, and uncontrol. Snakes, sinuous and fluid, emblems of both fertility and murderousness, lick the blood on their cheeks (lines 698, 767–68; cf. 102–3).[3] The women of the Chorus, the Bacchants who have followed Dionysus from Asia, seem more civilized and controlled and, up to a point, are so. But the lust for blood that surges ever more powerfully in their lyrics, their longing for "the delight of devouring raw meat" (line 139: my literal translation), their pitiless, avid response to the tragic events—these do not permit us to believe that we have found in them a safe and civilized Dionysianism.

Transgression, in fact, is everywhere. This play depicts a civilized city. The audience, seeing the drama at a solemn and orderly civic festival, might well expect to find in it a representation of the civilized as a distinctive category, contrasted sharply with the wild

---

[2] See Dodds (1960), 62–64; Kirk (1970), 24–25.

[3] For a comprehensive discussion of snake imagery in some classical authors, see B. M. W. Knox, "The Serpent and the Flame," *American Journal of Philology* 38 (1959), 379–400

or bestial. But if one looks for civilization and its protecting bound-
aries, one finds, instead, signs everywhere of the violation of bound-
aries. The fawn leaps the bounds erected by its human pursuers.
So, too, in many ways, this worship and these actions leap over the
bounds of civilized Greek life.[4] We hear of raw-eating, a violation
of civilized norms of sacrificial observance. We hear of women out-
side on the mountain, dancing unguarded, unwatched, their hair
loose in the wind—in extraordinary departures from usual Athenian
custom, according to which the woman's place was inside the house.
A mother transgresses the deepest law of civilized love and civil
society, killing her own child. And the straight, orderly structure of
declarative language is repeatedly transgressed as well—with cryptic
riddling ironies, mocking puns, double meanings. Even poetic
metricality is at one point transgressed. At a pivotal moment in their
exchange, just as Pentheus is ready to lead an armed assault against
the Maenads on the mountain, Dionysus stops him in his tracks,
turns him around, with an extrametrical "Ah." "Ah. But wouldn't
you like to see them on the mountain?" (lines 810–11). Summons
or caress, warning or cry of pleasure, the exclamation violates the
rhythm of the iambic trimeter dialogue in a striking and unusual
manner,[5] making the audience perceive these boundaries, too, as
fluid, these conventions as less than immutable.

Nor would these transgressions have been perceived by the au-
dience as simply the distant material of myth. For the *oreibasia*, the
dancing of women free and wild on the mountains in an organized
Dionysian ritual, was a recognized part of Athenian religion. At most
times, women in Athens were confined within the home to a degree
unusual even in the ancient Greek world. But through the religion
of Dionysus some of them could leave home, family, and even city
for a limited period every second year—to dance, to utter wild cries,
seeking contact with something beyond ordinary human life. Al-
though these rites almost certainly lacked many of the violent fea-

---

[4] See Segal (1982) for a comprehensive discussion of this theme.
[5] See Dodds (1960), 175; Segal (198), 286; Winnington-Ingram (1948), 102.
Williams's translation "Wait!" preserves well the force of the original.

tures of the rites described in the play, their incorporation within the city nonetheless involved the city in mystery and contradiction. By dramatizing these contradictions in a heightened and disturbing form, by emphasizing the foreignness of Dionysus and at the same time stressing the fact that he belongs in the Greek city and must be acknowledged, the play reflects on tensions within actual Athenian practices and norms—asking how the strange and foreign can reside at the heart of the civilized, asking whether the civilized is, after all, a distinctive category safely bounded off from the foreign, and even the bestial.

For it is not simply transgression of boundaries that we witness. It is the depiction of boundaries that might have seemed especially firm and reliable as fluid, mobile, suddenly shifting. What had seemed foul turns out to be beautiful. A killing that seemed glorious to the killers shifts and is seen as foul. Norms, constraints, shift as easily and silently as the snakes these women wear, sinuous and sudden. Nothing stands still for assessment.

II

These movements and tensions begin, as one considers them further, to map out a problematic cosmology, situating the human being fluidly and unclearly between the bestial and the divine—but not exactly in the usual or "simple" way.[6] The "simple" way—by which I mean a view that would have been generally prominent in the early religious education of the play's audience, and one that was becoming especially prominent in Euripides' time through the emphasis on it in the thought of sophists and philosophers—does indeed identify the human as a being whose nature it is to be situated between the beast on the one hand and the god on the other, and who derives its characteristic form of life from this in-between status, as well as from the boundaries that mark off its special position.

---

[6] For more extensive discussion of these issues, see M. Nussbaum, *The Fragility of Goodness: Luck and Ethics in Greek Tragedy and Philosophy* (Cambridge, 1986), with references; and Nussbaum, "Transcending Humanity," in *Love's Knowledge: Essays on Philosophy and Literature* (New York, 1990).

The "simple" way presents the following picture. At the top of nature, so to speak (and also literally), are the gods, beings who are unlimited, immortal, blessed, perfect. They possess reason and language, and there are no limits to their reason's efficacy, either external or internal. At the bottom are the beasts, without language, without reason, therefore without structure and order to their lives, finite and mortal, creatures of appetite and circumstance. In the middle are human beings. These beings share with the gods language and reason, but on the other hand are mortal and finite like the beasts; and like beasts they have, in connection with their finitude, an insistent bodily and appetitive nature. They are resourceful, but needy and unsafe.

This simple schematic picture is common enough; and it has deep roots. Thus even when the gods are portrayed, as they frequently are in myth, as subject to various human weaknesses and limitations, it can be powerfully argued, as it is by thinkers such as Xenophanes and Plato, that, strictly speaking, such portrayals, however entertaining they may be, are inconsistent with the city's deepest beliefs about what gods really are and what befits them. Thus Plato's Socrates, in the *Republic*, Books II–III, has an easy time convincing the conventionally educated Glaucon that something is amiss with stories that show the gods as limited by fear or need. Such stories, Socrates suggests—and I think correctly—conflict not only with the conclusions of Platonic philosophy, but also with one very deep strand in ordinary Athenian beliefs and conceptions concerning what is appropriate to divinity.

Frequently, however, in complex traditions of both reflection and storytelling, this "simple" view, while maintained, is also made deeper and more complicated. The more complex suggestion—which one finds already in authors such as Homer, Heraclitus, and Sophocles, and which reaches its most extensive development in the thought of Aristotle—is that the human being is not simply a stapling together of two unrelated groups of traits, the godlike abilities and the bestial limits. The two "pieces" respond to and shape each other, producing something different and altogether new. Reason responds to need and need is educated by reason. The product of this inter-action is social morality.[7] Animals are incapable of forming a civi-lized city and of living according to the constraints of virtues such as justice, moderation, and courage. They are incapable of educating their passions so as to develop these virtues as stable traits of char-acter. They are not, therefore, responsive to the claims and the needs of others. Gods, on the other side, being nonfinite, have no need of the moral virtues. These do not apply to their unlimited form of life; their logic would not be evident there. A being with no limits cannot run a race; the logic of that physical exercise is not applicable where no limits are to be found. So, too, an immortal and nonfinite being cannot have courage: for there are no really serious risks to run. Nor does moderation seem to have a point, since there is no deter-mining what the right indulgence of appetite is when there are no ill health and no disease. Nor, as Aristotle observed, would justice have any point in a life in which there are no needs and no shortages. "It would be ridiculous," he wrote, "to imagine the gods paying back deposits and so forth."[8] This means that the gods are likely to lack understanding of the role and point of these human virtues in human life, and to lack empathy with the struggle against limitation and need that is connected with them.

When one reflects this way, the "top" and the "bottom" con-verge. God seems to have something in common with beast. As Aristotle observes, neither is, fundamentally, a social being, and neither really has the moral virtues: "For one is above the virtues, and the deficiency of the other is a different sort of thing from ethical deficiency."[9] The fact that neither is a social being involves, among other things, the idea that neither fully comprehends or responds to human need and suffering: the one because it lacks all under-standing, the other because it is beyond suffering and has never had

---

[7] See Nussbaum, *Fragility*, chap. 12; and "Aristotle on Human Nature and the Foundation of Ethics," forthcoming in a volume on the philosophy of Bernard Wil-liams, ed. J. E. G. Altham and R. Harrison (Cambridge, 1990).

[8] Aristotle, *Nicomachean Ethics*, 1178b10–16

[9] Ibid., 1145a25 ff.; cf. *Politics*, 1253a27 ff.

experience of a limited life. This complex idea makes its first appearance in the Greek tradition in Homer, leading to a depiction of the gods as rather light and frivolous beings, lacking the ethical seriousness that comes to mortals through their constant engagement with death and other limits, incapable therefore of true courage, grief, or risk-taking loyalty. (There are exceptions, clearly—as in Zeus's grief for the death of his son Sarpedon, branded by Plato as most ungodlike, or in various cases where the gods experience limits in relation to one another. But in general the contrast between the divine and mortal worlds is sharp, given the conventions of an anthropomorphic theology.) The same problem appears even more prominently in certain elements of tragedy: for example, at the ending of Sophocles' *Women of Trachis*, where Hyllus contrasts the pity and fellow-thought-and-feeling (*suggnōmosunē*) of the human world with the sheer thoughtlessness (*agnōmosunē*) of the gods, saying that this divinely caused human suffering is "pitiable for us, shameful for them."[10] Finally, such reflections are prominently developed in Aristotle's thought about what it is to be a social being. And Aristotle refers frequently to elements of traditional belief in his arguments for the conclusion that the human being, and the human being alone, is social and ethical. Throughout this complex tradition, then, the gods, insofar as they lack ethical seriousness and compassion for suffering, touch hands with the bestial.

The Bacchae explores this complex idea and complicates it further, situating god and beast so close to one another that it is frequently impossible to distinguish them. Dionysus, a god, can take shape as a snake, a bull, a lion (line 1018). Exalted and exalting, he totally lacks compassion; and his vengeance is not tempered by any sensitivity to the suffering he inflicts. He and his followers are somehow lifted above the human world in the ecstasy of their oneness with nature. But, being above the moral constraints of the human world, they also seem to fall below it, into the wild callous-

---

[10] For a discussion of this passage and its relation to these themes, see Nussbaum, "Transcending."

ness of the bestial. Dionysus is lofty, serene, above it all, always smiling; but by the same token, in his lofty indifference to pity and even to justice (see sections V and VI in this Introduction), he falls beneath norms that the city prizes, and prizes with good reason.

In the middle of this cosmos sits the human world, a world of social morality, of pity and compassion, of fellow feeling with other mortal intelligent beings. But the human realm is not shown, here, as self-sufficient. Its walls are highly porous: influences flow in from the other realms, and human beings make strange and sudden exits into them. What is stranger still is that, apparently, their full humanity depends on these exits. Pentheus, obsessed with limits and enclosures, believes he has succeeded in bounding off the human city from these strange external influences. But he fails: Dionysus conquers his mind and takes his life. And we see, moreover, that his obsession with enclosure has, even before Dionysus' punishment, made of Pentheus a fierce and bestial creature. So if human beings close themselves off from Dionysus' call, they apparently become less than fully human. But if they listen to Dionysus, this carries, it seems, the risk of another sort of beastliness. Humanness appears as an unstable and temporary achievement, poised among dangers of many kinds. And the deep question of the play is: What is a human morality, and what is its relation to the acknowledgment of Dionysus? Can there be a life that repudiates this religion and also remains moral, civilized, and fully human? Can there be a life that accepts and lives by this religion and also remains moral, civilized, and fully human? (And who are the spectators of this play, seated in an apparently civilized manner in the theater of Dionysus?) We shall return to these questions in section VI—not necessarily to provide straightforward answers.

III

In 408 B.C., Euripides left Athens for the court of Archelaus, ruler of Macedon. His career had been a long and distinguished one. Though he had won the first prize in the competitions of the tragic festivals surprisingly rarely, his popularity with audiences was great, as one can see from *The Frogs* of Aristophanes, a comic drama produced in 405. Here the comic hero (none other than Dionysus) reads Euripides with enthusiasm and assumes that either he or Aeschylus will be the poet to be resurrected from the underworld to give advice to the city in its time of difficulty. (Sophocles is given the same high rank, but is judged to be too serene a character to want to leave the underworld.) The very prominence of Euripides as a target of comic lampooning (sometimes taken as evidence of unpopularity) testifies to his preeminence. Thus there seems to be no reason to believe, with some scholars,[11] that he left Athens out of bitterness and disappointment. Athens was in a depressed and exhausted condition near the end of the long Peloponnesian War, and beset by domestic political tensions. Archelaus' court offered a luxurious way of life and enthusiastic patronage. Many other first-rate artists and poets found the prospect irresistible—among them the tragic poet Agathon and the painter Zeuxis. Archelaus is depicted in an extremely unfriendly light in Plato's *Gorgias*, where he is made the paradigm of the unjust, ruthless, and unrepentant tyrant. But to artists he was a civilized and lavish supporter.

During his stay in Macedon, Euripides wrote a play called *Archelaus*, about an ancestor of the king, and a number of other works. At his death in 406 (at the age of around seventy) he left three unproduced plays, which were later staged at Athens by one of his sons. The group, which won the first prize, probably in 405, included two plays that survive: *Iphigenia at Aulis* and *The Bacchae*.

It has sometimes been suggested that the wild landscape of Macedon and its connection with archaic traditions inspired Euripides to turn his thoughts to the theme of Dionysian transcendence and unity with nature.[12] But such biographical suggestions tend to be superficial and unreliable. (Roux compares the effect of Macedonian landscapes on Euripides to the effect of Niagara Falls on Chateaubriand—a comparison that comments on itself, since it is

---

[11] For example, Arrowsmith (1959), Roux (1970–72). Even Dodds (1960), xxxix, subscribes to a version of this thesis

[12] See especially Roux (1970), introduction.

now generally believed that Chateaubriand never saw Niagara
Falls.) Dionysian themes were prominent in ancient tragedy: Aes-
chylus wrote two trilogies on such subjects.[13] And Euripides' own
career shows a continuous interest in the themes treated in *The
Bacchae*. An early lost play, *The Cretans*, dealt with ecstatic religion.
Its surviving fragment mentions Zagreus (a form of Dionysus), feasts
of raw flesh, Curetes (mythical Cretan divinities, associated with
stories of Dionysus' youth), and Bacchants. The *Hippolytus*, pro-
duced in 428, is very close to *The Bacchae* in its portrayal both of
the violence of erotic desire and of the impoverished character of a
life that attempts to close it off completely. The *Helen* (412) contains
an ode dealing with the mysteries of the Mountain Mother. *The
Bacchae* seems uncharacteristic, calling for some special biograph-
ical interpretation, only if one accepts an account of Euripides' ca-
reer such as the one given by Nietzsche, who claimed that until he
wrote this one play Euripides had been the poet of the supremacy
of the intellect, crisp and optimistic, totally insensitive to the power
of irrational forces in human life, and to their beauty. But this inter-
pretation cannot survive a scrutiny of the earlier plays. For even
where rational debate is given prominence (as, for example, in *The
Trojan Women*), it is usually shown to be powerless against other
darker forces such as love, desire, and greed.

The language of *The Bacchae* is, however, rather unusual within
Euripides' work as we know it. Although the iambics of the dialogue
sections show metrical tendencies that link them unmistakably with
the other late plays, the style and diction are in many places archaic,
solemn, almost Aeschylean in their formality. Gilbert Murray called
The Bacchae "the most formal Greek play known to us."[14] Its "se-
verity of form" (Dodds)[15] is in striking tension with its strange and
passionate content. Its lyrics have little of the concern with deco-
ration that marks a number of Euripides' later dramas. The use of
refrains links them with cult hymns, as do some of the meters se-

[13] See Dodds (1960), xxviii–xxxiii; Kirk (1970), 2–3.
[14] Quoted in Dodds (1960), xxxvi
[15] Ibid , xxxviii

lected. In one dialogue section (lines 604–41) the play revives (like several other late plays of Euripides) the trochaic tetrameter, a very old tragic meter, which combines an archaizing effect with rapid light movement, as the god describes the ease with which he has slipped away from Pentheus and confounded human attempts to bind him.

IV

The nineteen extant plays of Euripides (out of an original total of ninety-two) survive in two groups of manuscripts deriving from two ancient editions. One group, annotated with scholia, derives from an ancient Roman school edition of selected plays. The second group, without scholia, is part of a comprehensive collection of Euripides' works in alphabetical order; it contains plays whose titles begin with the letters epsilon, eta, iota, and kappa. By far the largest number of surviving manuscripts contain the "select plays." Only two manuscripts contain the alphabetical group; these combine them with the select plays and *The Bacchae*. *The Bacchae* is present only in this combined edition. In fact, only lines 1–755 survive in one manuscript; for the other half of the play we are dependent on a single manuscript, and not a terribly good one. Because *The Bacchae* does not belong alphabetically with the E–K group, and for a number of other reasons as well, scholars have concluded that it was originally transmitted as a part of the "select" group, but that it was probably the last play in that group and therefore was mutilated at an early stage of transmission, as frequently happens to the ends of manuscripts, and was later often omitted altogether.

The latter part of the play seems to contain two gaps. These are not indicated in the surviving manuscript and therefore must date back to the mutilation of some ancestor. One gap is after line 1300, where Agave's question goes unanswered. Another one, apparently longer, occurs after line 1329, where the end of Agave's speech and the beginning of the god's appearance and prophecy are lacking. Fragments, and the general contents, of the lost material can be reconstructed with the help of the *Christus Patiens*, a peculiar twelfth-century poem on the Passion of Christ, which is composed out of a collage of quotations from various ancient tragedies. One section contains numerous bits from *The Bacchae*, and some of its pieces have been identified as belonging to the lost portion. These pieces show that the body of Pentheus is reassembled by Cadmus and Agave, and that she laments over each limb. The scene would have given considerable weight and emphasis to this activity of mourning and reconstruction. Williams's lines filling the gap are based upon these fragments, although the original may very well have had a longer treatment of the same material.

v

Just as Dionysus has many shapes, so the play has meant many things to many people. From its first performance until the present day, it has remained among the most popular of Euripides' works. In antiquity it was one of the most frequently performed tragedies, both as a whole and in extracts. Its performance history has the same bizarre and unexpected character as the play itself. The emperor Nero loved the role of Agave and acted it in public performance— a strangely significant choice, in a career marked by obsession with contriving the murder of his own mother. Plutarch's *Life of Crassus* relates an earlier story of even greater strangeness. In 53 B.C., at the court of Artavasdes, king of Armenia, the king ordered a performance of the play to celebrate the marriage of his sister to Pacorus, son of the Parthian king. (This wedding signaled his own shift of loyalty from Rome to Parthia.) Meanwhile, the Parthians had dealt the Roman army a crushing defeat at the battle of Carrhae, with Armenian assistance. The head of the Roman general Crassus was brought to Artavasdes during the performance. The well-known actor Jason of Tralles, who was acting the role of Agave, seized the severed head and played the scene with it, earning a rich reward. Perhaps it is not surprising that even now, in less dramatic and more local ways, production of the play continues to be linked with sudden upheavals and with the power of the unexpected. In 1969, for example, in New York, the radical theater group led by critic and director Richard Schechner chose *The Bacchae* as the first work for a theater in which nudity, ritual, and audience participation were explored with famous and controversial effect. In the production of *Dionysus in '69* and in Schechner's writings,[16] the play became linked with both the "sexual revolution" and the opposition to the Vietnam War. Pentheus was seen as a figure of the establishment, rigid and militaristic, the opponent of a free, sensual life. Thus the play became, for many who were aware of that production, an emblem of that strange and contradictory time, in which the demand for peace and freedom was accompanied, frequently, with violence and disorder; in which compassion was sometimes strangely mingled with a lack of sensitivity to one's own excess and cruelty.

Written interpretations of the play are enormously diverse and contradictory. An examination of some of the most prominent trends in the past one hundred and fifty years or so shows how many-sided Dionysus and the play actually are—and shows, too, how dangerous it is to focus on only a single aspect, believing that one has uncovered the whole.

This examination can begin with Friedrich Nietzsche, whose description of Dionysus and the Dionysian, in *The Birth of Tragedy* and in other writings,[17] is as perceptive as his overall portrait of Euripides is deficient. According to this portrait, the Dionysian is a universal "tendency" in human life: the tendency to move and act in accordance with irrational forces, especially the force of erotic desire (it is closely modeled on Schopenhauer's *Wille*.) This drive seeks the transgressing and even the complete effacing of clear, distinct boundaries; it seeks, as well, the obliteration of the individuality of the subject, in a merging oneness with nature. Intoxication is a frequent symptom and concomitant of Dionysian experience; its characteristic artistic expression is in the fluid movement of the dance. Opposed to the Dionysian is the "Apollinian" tendency, the

---

[16] See Schechner (1969).

[17] Nietzsche (1872); other important discussions of Dionysus and the Dionysian are in the posthumously edited fragments: see *The Will to Power* (1883–88), trans W. Kaufmann and R. Hollingdale (New York, 1967).

propensity to approach the world with cool reason, carving it up and making clear distinctions. Whereas the Apollinian person is static and contemplative, the person under the sway of Dionysus is always on the move and makes contact with the world through movement and touch, rather than through thought. One is a pure reason, the other a dancing body.

It was Nietzsche's view that these two tendencies had to be combined if any fully human life was to be achieved. Human beings need the order and discipline of Apollo, but also the vitality and erotic energy of Dionysus. And in his view Greek tragedy worked out a remarkable artistic combination of the two tendencies, with its interest in reasoning and in ethical order, with its affirmation, through music and dance, of the strength and value of the animal side of human life. Nietzsche's own time, as he saw it, had a particular need of recovering this Dionysian element, since Christianity had taught the modern European to despise the body and its energy.

For this reason, Nietzsche welcomed *The Bacchae* as a triumphant affirmation of the power of the irrational in human life. Although, as I have said, he held that Euripides was, through most of his career, a chilly rationalist, a follower of "Socratic optimism" hostile to emotion and desire, he saw this last play as Euripides' deathbed conversion, a final sudden acknowledgment of the divinity he had long scorned. And Nietzsche himself, seeing asceticism and otherworldliness as the chief enemies of human flourishing in his time, embraced the play and its Dionysus, seeing in that religion a possible antidote to modern ills.

This positive assessment of Dionysus was quickly countered by a group of critics who focused on the excessive and cruel character of Dionysus' actions, the fanatical and uncritical behavior of his adherents. Nietzsche's great enemy, the classical scholar Wilamowitz, was a major exponent of this line. An eccentric variant on this position was proposed early in this century by two British scholars, Verrall and Norwood.[18] According to Verrall's influential books *Eu-*

---

[18] Wilamowitz-Moellendorff (1923), Verrall (1895 and 1910), Norwood (1908); Norwood recanted his earlier view in (1954). See the critical discussion of rationalist views in Dodds (1960), xlviii–l

ripides the Rationalist (1895) and *The Bacchants of Euripides and Other Essays* (1910), there is no discontinuity whatever in Euripides' career (the early part of which Verrall paints much as Nietzsche does). From first to last he is the Socratic defender of reason against superstition and convention. *The Bacchae* is an exposé of the irrationality of ecstatic religion. According to Verrall, the audience would recognize that the stranger is simply a fake, a charmer, no god at all. And they would conclude that all the play's characters, with the exception of the heroic Pentheus, are his dupes. In fact, in the play as staged, the audience would have recognized that none of the miraculous events described actually took place. The "palace miracle" would have been seen as a manifestation of collective hysteria.

Both the Nietzschean view and the "rationalist" view bring out aspects of the play that have genuine importance. But both fail to be convincing overall. Nietzsche's theory of the deathbed conversion is implausible, as I argued earlier. And his celebration of Dionysus does not, as we shall see, fully recognize the ethical complexities of the play's assessment. But his sensitive portrayal of the impulse to Dionysian worship does justice to the play's portrait of the beauty and force of the irrational, and of the poetry that these forces write; and this the rationalist interpreters simply miss. It is impossible that an Athenian audience, gathered at a solemn festival of Dionysus, could have seen the play as a denial of the god's divinity and a simple condemnation of the cult. The extraordinary beauty of the choral lyrics, the sense of wonder and strangeness that fill the drama as a whole, are completely ignored in this reading. Nor can Pentheus plausibly be seen as a heroic defender of reason. For the play depicts him as tyrannical, bestial in his rage, rigid and unreflective, concealing beneath his bluster the very desires he denounces, desires made sneaking and ugly by repression. In the words of E. R. Dodds, Euripides "has given him the foolish racial pride of a Hermione and the sexual curiosity of a Peeping Tom. It is not thus that martyrs of enlightenment are represented."[19] As to the sug-

---

[19] Dodds (1960), xliii.

gestion that the miracles are fakes, this can surely be dismissed. It is one of the firmest conventions of the ancient theater—in which much of the relevant action takes place elsewhere and is described—that the audience is to believe reports of offstage events. And the play, on these terms, would have to be regarded as a disastrous failure, since no spectator guessed its true significance for two thousand years.

In this century, interpreters have usually avoided these two extremes; but related differences of emphasis remain. E. R. Dodds, in his distinguished commentary (1944, second ed. 1960) and in his important book *The Greeks and the Irrational* (1951),[20] argued for the great importance of the Dionysian, and of irrational desire and emotion generally, in Greek society and its views of the good human life. He saw the play as proclaiming the divinity of a Dionysus who is "beyond good and evil,"[21] who cannot and should not be judged by human ethical standards, but must simply be acknowledged. Dodds developed with rigorous scholarship the best features of the Nietzschean reading, discarding the conversion story and recognizing to a greater extent than Nietzsche the moral ambiguity of Dionysus' actions. He is a god and exemplifies divine wisdom; but he is also heartless. He combines "joy and horror, insight and madness, innocent gaiety and dark cruelty."[22] Although Pentheus is no hero, his fate does inspire pity, since what he suffers is disproportionate to his offense.

But in the end, Dodds sees the play as optimistic about the relationship between the Dionysian and human morality. For his interpretation makes central the idea of repression and the "return of the repressed"; and it strongly contrasts the two groups of Bacchants. Pentheus and the Theban Bacchants have denied Dionysus and repressed in themselves the forces he represents. Therefore the return of these repressed forces brings with it a madness that is devastating: for Pentheus, delusion and the loss of self-respect; for

[20] Dodds (1951), 64–101.
[21] Dodds (1960). xlv.
[22] Ibid , xliv.

the Theban women, murderous excess, "raw" hysteria. By contrast, Dodds argues, the women of the Chorus, Asian Bacchants who have accepted and followed Dionysus, exemplify a "white maenadism" that combines the beautiful and invigorating features of Dionysian worship with an avoidance of its excesses. Dodds concludes:

> . . . the "moral" of the *Bacchae* is that we ignore at our peril the demand of the human spirit for Dionysiac experience. For those who do not close their minds against it such experience can be a deep source of spiritual power and *eudaimonia*. But those who repress the demand in themselves or refuse its satisfaction to others transform it by their act into a power of disintegration and destruction, a blind natural force that sweeps away the innocent with the guilty. When that has happened, it is too late to reason or to plead: in man's justice there is room for pity, but there is none in the justice of Nature; to our "Ought" its sufficient reply is the simple "Must"; we have no choice but to accept that reply and to endure it as we may.[23]

This interpretation goes a long way toward a recognition of the play's tensions and complexities. But in this rather too comfortable conclusion, Dodds, too, oversimplifies. Dionysus' excessive rage is seen not only in the women on the mountain (who, besides, are not, in general, "raw" in their hysteria, and whose chastity and order-liness are stressed).[24] It is seen, as well, in the blood lust of the women of the Chorus. True, they do not rip people apart before the eyes of the audience. But this would have been impossible on the Greek stage. They do, however, speak of violent and transgres-sive acts with enthusiasm: of the joy of raw-eating, the hunting down of the enemy. In connection with Pentheus' death, they make ex-traordinary use of the language of victory in the contest (line 1162), even of the solemn victory hymn (line 1161)—here exactly echoing the language of Agave on the mountain (line 1147). If this is, to use Dodds's phrase, "white maenadism," it is white not in the sense of

---

[23] Ibid., xlv.
[24] See especially the speech of the Messenger at lines 677 ff.

"innocent," but white as Moby Dick is white—strange, ambiguous, sinister as well as beautiful. The two groups of Bacchants are a necessary feature of the plot; necessary, as well, because the Chorus, once in place, cannot exit, and yet actions of the sort the play depicts cannot be shown upon the tragic stage. The groups are distinguished: one has chosen to follow Dionysus, the other is the victim of a punishment. But they are not set apart as neatly, in the play's description of their attitudes and behavior, as Dodds suggests.

Nor does Dionysus' rage limit itself to his opponents. The pious and deferential Cadmus is stricken at the end, and the entire house ruined. The smiling mask of the god (see line 1021) takes on, as the play progresses, an increasingly sinister significance, until the audience would be likely to share the judgment of Cadmus: that the vengeance meted out by the god was "if just, still excessive" (line 1249: my own literal translation), and that "Gods should not resemble mortals in anger" (line 1348).

These features of the play have been well brought out in some recent work on the play: especially in G. S. Kirk's admirable commentary (1970, 1979)[25] and in C. P. Segal's comprehensive and valuable book *Dionysiac Poetics and Euripides' Bacchae* (1982).[26] They were already well described in R. P. Winnington-Ingram's classic study *Euripides and Dionysus: An Interpretation of the* Bacchae (1948),[27] still among the best accounts of the play as a whole. A related account is given in René Girard's *Violence and the Sacred* (1972),[28] which argues that the attempt at a displacement of violence in the play remains ambivalent and that the audience would remain confused and disturbed, feeling that peace had not been fully restored by Pentheus' death.

Recent work has shed new light as well on three aspects of the

---

[25] Kirk (1970, repr. 1979); page numbers are cited from the former edition.

[26] Segal (1982); see also Segal (1977, 1978, 1986), Henrichs (1982).

[27] Winnington-Ingram (1948, repr. 1969). Despite the excellence of Winnington-Ingram's overall account of the play, he appears too eager to find in it a "solution" to the problems it represents. Thus he is led to give Cadmus and Tiresias, whom Euripides surely portrays as comic figures, a central and very positive role, claiming that Tiresias represents the solution that Athens would find to the tensions manifested in Dionysian religion, and in the drama.

[28] Girard (translation 1977, originally 1972).

play that had been less thoroughly studied in the earlier literature: the connection between the play's Dionysian myth and the historical Dionysian cult, the psychological portraiture, and the play's self-conscious theatricality. It is well beyond my scope in this introduction to describe the current state of scholarship with regard to the historical cult of Dionysus at Athens and elsewhere in the Greek world—all the more since one important result of that scholarship is a new awareness of the danger of basing such a historical account on a reading of *The Bacchae*. Albert Henrichs and other scholars have insisted that one must not hastily conflate the Dionysus myth, as depicted in this play and in other literary works, with the actual Dionysus cult.[29] Henrichs, in particular, has insisted on recognizing the diversity of Dionysian cultic practices in different regions and at different times, and on "the fundamental difference between his [Dionysus'] mythic and cultic manifestations."[30] *The Bacchae*, Henrichs argues, portrays a "worst-case scenario characterized by a disturbed relationship between men and gods, and by the temporary suspension of normal civic and social mechanisms, including cult."[31] This does not, of course, imply that the play contains no commentary upon the civilized city and its usual practices. What it does imply is that an attempt to understand these actual practices in their ordinary form must rely on other kinds of evidence. The evidence of myth and cult together does in the end, Henrichs argues, provide a "consistent if contradictory" picture of Dionysus in all his polarities and strange complexities. But one should not assume, as Dodds tended to, that the play is simply continuous with actual cultic practices.[32]

[29] See Henrichs, especially (1979, 1982, 1984a). Henrichs also emphasizes the multiplicity and complexity of Dionysian cultic manifestations: "The so-called 'religion of Dionysus' is a convenient modern abstraction, the sum total of the god's numerous facets, symbols and cults. Dionysus had no central priesthood, no canonical books, and not even a panhellenic shrine of his own. His cults were regional and emphasized different aspects of the god" (Henrichs [1982], 151–52).

[30] Henrichs (1990).

[31] Ibid.

[32] Although Dodds to some extent qualifies this on pp. xxii–xxiii, where he observes that the play responds to a period at which Athens is being "invaded" by a multitude of foreign cults, such as those of Cybele, Bendis, Attis, Adonis, and Sabazius, and incorporates certain Oriental elements.

In one particular detail of considerable importance, Dodds's interpretation of Dionysian worship has been successfully criticized. Dodds believed that *The Bacchae* provided evidence for the presence of a "male celebrant" at the otherwise female rituals of mountain-dancing.[33] He attached considerable importance to this and gave it a large place in his historical reconstruction of Dionysian religion. Through the prestige of Dodds's work, the suggestion has been taken up by others. Dodds's idea was a daring innovation. Prior to that time, historians of Greek religion had maintained, on the basis of both inscriptional and textual evidence about cultic practices, that the bands of Maenads who worshipped Dionysus by dancing at night on the mountain were composed entirely of women, and that the only male role in this particular manifestation of Dionysian religion was the limited and passive role of the *gunaikonomos*, or "women's guardian," who kept a watchful eye on the Maenads' conduct from a distance, but was almost certainly barred from the rites themselves. Males clearly worshipped Dionysus too, but in different ways: above all through drinking parties, which probably included singing and possibly some dancing, but not outdoor dancing of the Maenadic variety. Dodds's proposal thus went against a well-supported tradition according to which the god's gifts to the two sexes were kept sharply distinct. He did not base his claim upon the action of *The Bacchae*, nor could he have: for it is stressed that the women, contrary to Pentheus' charges, neither drink wine nor mingle with men; and Cadmus and Tiresias, though they do head off to the mountain to dance, cannot have joined the women, since they learn of Pentheus' fate only after their return. Instead, Dodds appealed to two passages in the first chorus (lines 114 ff. and 132 ff.), passages that are textually corrupt and difficult to construe. Henrichs has shown that readings that are probably superior in any case from a textual point of view do not introduce the so-called male celebrant, or male leader of the female rites—for whose existence there is otherwise

[33] Dodds (1940), 170, n. 71, Dodds (1960), 82 ff., 85–88.

no evidence in either myth or cult.[34] It is the god himself whom the women believe to be leading them—as Williams's translation, following Henrichs's suggestions, implies.

Another recent group of writings, loosely psychoanalytic in orientation, has focused on the play's depiction of Pentheus' complex psychology, and on the shifts in Agave's self-awareness during what has come to be called the "psychoanalysis scene."[35] Though one may dispute the merits of using one or another particular psychoanalytic vocabulary to interpret ancient tragedy, and though it is very important not to endow dreams and fantasies with a significance that they could not have had in Greek society of that time, the fact remains that the hidden workings of fear and fantasy are prominent themes in ancient literature and even philosophy. (Epicureanism, for example, has an elaborate theory of the behavior produced by an unconscious fear of death.) And in general the idea of hidden impulses, and also of a therapy that works on the soul through the word, are ideas older than most formal philosophy and very important in literary works of many kinds. Thus critics whose interest in such phenomena has been stimulated by contemporary psychoanalytic theory have been able to advance our understanding of the portrayals of Pentheus and Agave. Pentheus' fantasies of an infantile dependence on his mother prompt a wish that he could have the "luxury" of being held once again, like a baby, in her arms.[36] This significant and frequently neglected passage has been justly emphasized by psychoanalytical critics. Like Hippolytus, Pentheus proves unable to negotiate successfully the transition from childhood to male adulthood. His struggle against the bull (lines 616 ff.) ap-

---

[34] Henrichs (1984a); on Attic Maenads, see Henrichs (1978), 152–55; Henrichs (1982) points out that Dionysian groups admitting both sexes together began to be in evidence by the fifth century (see, for example, Herodotus 4.78–80); but the members of these groups are not Maenads in the ritual sense. During the Hellenistic period, the distinction between ritual Maenadism and less restricted forms of Dionysianism began to be blurred (Henrichs [1982], 147).

[35] For a good general discussion of psychoanalytical readings, see Segal (1986), "Pentheus and Hippolytus"; other prominent examples of such readings are Sale (1972) and Devereux (1970); see also Simon (1978).

[36] See Segal, "Pentheus."

pears to be, as well, a violent struggle against a part of his own nature. His alternation between excessive masculine aggressiveness and an exaggerated feminine passivity suggests a deep ambivalence about masculine maturity. And this rejection of adulthood is plausibly linked to his preference for voyeurism, his interest in witnessing sexual acts without being ensnared in the complexities of his own desires. His death—head carried in the "enfolding embrace" (line 1277) of his mother—is an ironic fulfillment of his wish. Related complexities are illuminated in psychoanalytic readings of Agave's recognition scene, itself an example of the ancient interest in psychotherapy.

Such psychoanalytical readings, when carefully worked out, are in no way incompatible with readings (such as mine in this introduction) that emphasize the socially constructed elements of the play's language, focusing on its exploration of historically constituted categories and polarities. The best psychoanalytic readings look at the play's language carefully in its own right, and in its own historical context, rather than dogmatically imposing an alien jargon. And the best readings of the "social-constructionist" variety are alert to nuances in the depictions of individual characters. They are also sensitive to the ways in which the polarities that structure the discourse of a group (for example, the opposition between god and beast, on which I have focused here) explore deep human responses to widely shared human problems and are not just strange discursive idiosyncrasies of merely local interest.

The drama has always been studied as drama, in a sense. But recently scholars have begun to focus more intently than before on its self-consciousness about the theater and about its own character as theater. The fact that it is a play about Dionysus performed in a theater of Dionysus is obvious enough; and yet it deserves emphasis. For in many ways the play itself draws attention to its theatrical character—portraying Dionysus as a consummate actor/playwright who assumes many forms, and whose smiling mask takes on changing meanings; commenting on the joy of the very type of dancing and singing the Chorus is at that moment performing; focusing the attention of the audience on scenes of transformation, costuming,

and illusion. Both Helene Foley and Charles Segal[37] have argued
that in this way the play leads the audience to reflect about the
theater as a civilized yet Dionysian institution—and therefore to
pose, urgently, the question that dominates the play: Can Dionysus
really become civilized?

VI

What is the play's answer to this question? On the one hand, Pen-
theus, as I have said, is not a heroic figure; and his psychological
oddness undercuts his claim to represent the position of pure reason.
On the other hand, Dodds's view, according to which the play offers
a clear paradigm of civilized ecstasy, seems unjustified in the light
of the play's complexities. And Pentheus' beardless youth makes us
pity him even as we condemn him. One cannot help feeling that
the responses of Nietzsche and Dodds, affirming an unequivocally
positive role for Dionysus in human life, were products of the fact
that both lived in societies in which religious observance, and society
in general, had become (in their view) lifeless and passionless. What
was needed, it seemed, was a new infusion of erotic/religious energy;
and it seemed plausible to believe that the bounds of civilized mo-
rality could contain and shape that energy. To a contemporary
reader, on the other hand, such optimism is likely to seem naïve
and facile; nor do the terrible excesses that take place in the play
appear distant or easily avoidable. So we can hardly help noticing
the fact that the play does not portray the religion of Dionysus as
safe or tame or civilized, even when accepted, but rather as trans-
gressive and heartless—and yet also as necessary, beautiful, divine.
This is what is hard to comprehend, and even harder not to
repudiate.

Three prominent patterns of imagery that run throughout the
play make the dimensions of the problem clearer: imagery of hunt-
ing, animal imagery, and imagery of gender and gender reversal.[38]
Pentheus begins by displaying himself as the hunter, trapping and

[37] Foley (1985), Segal (1982).
[38] On all these, see Segal (1982) and also (1978).

binding his prey:[39] "I'll track them down," he announces (lines 226–28), planning to snare them in "nets of iron" (line 231). Dionysus makes his first appearance as "the prey you wanted," "the animal" (lines 434–36); and Pentheus rejoices: "He's in my net" (line 451). But this initial situation is reversed, as Dionysus slips out of Pentheus' grasp, leaving him to bind a bull instead (lines 618–20). And shortly: "He's in the net" (line 848); and the serene women of the Chorus imagine themselves, at once, as animals escaping from the hunt and as partisans of the divine hunter (lines 862 ff., see section I of this introduction). Their next ode calls on the "hounds of madness" to track and kill the enemy (lines 977 ff). This symmetry is aesthetically and dramatically satisfying; at the same time, it is morally disturbing. For, as Cadmus says, gods should not resemble mortals in their anger. The symmetry between Pentheus (portrayed throughout as animal-like and excessive in his rage) and the god is too much symmetry. Doubles in apparent age and in parentage, descendants of the dragon's teeth, the two are doubles in ferocity as well. The one has the excuses of youth, inexperience, and passionate involvement; the detached cruelty of the other hunter does not call forth pity, except for his victims.

The animal imagery, however, makes it clear that the situation is more complex still. For comparisons of Pentheus to a beast (lines 537 ff.; cf. lines 619–20), complemented by references to his infantile character, remind us that full adult humanity cannot be attained in a life that resolutely closes off Dionysus and the impulses—erotic, ecstatic—that he brings to human life. (Hippolytus, too, closing off the influence of Aphrodite, becomes a rigid, incomplete figure.) So the risks that Dionysian worship brings with it cannot be avoided altogether; they are there in humanity itself, and the only way to avoid them is by a violent suppression. But the dissolution of humanity that certain Dionysian excesses bring is accomplished all the more surely by a life that suppresses and denies him. On the other

---

[39] See also Nussbaum, *Fragility*, chap. 1. In two cases in this discussion ("nets of iron" and "full of desire"), I have substituted my own literal version for Williams's more idiomatic translations

hand, Dionysus *is* both beast and god. The risk involved in acknowledging him is a risk not just of vulnerability to strange influences; it is a risk of becoming, oneself, a beast. With its reference to the laws of Dionysian worship as firmly fixed in nature, the Chorus suggests that there is in humanity a permanent element that both fulfills and completes humanity and also seeks humanity's extinction, the extinction of the boundaries of civilization, the boundaries of ethical discourse. We cannot and should not, being humans, close ourselves off from that element; for it will rage out of us and devour us. But if we open ourselves to accept it, then it may also rage out and devour us. There seems to be little hope of remaining safely, stably human and moral, proud in our ethical security. This may be why the Chorus so strangely links ecstasy and transcendence with the praise of moderation and keeping one's place: because to know that we are followers of and constituted by that ecstasy is to know as well that we cannot firmly claim a dignity that we might have wished to claim for ourselves: the dignity of reason, of firm morality. We keep our place—not as simply different from the divine, but also as its subjects, subject to its beauty and its danger.

The play's remarkable imagery of gender reversal deepens this point. Pentheus begins as an active, aggressively masculine figure according to Athenian conventions of masculinity, in which the most important thing in maleness is activity and the avoidance of passivity.[40] He mocks the soft, sinuous, feminine form of Dionysus (pages 453 ff.): his long curls, "full of desire," his untanned skin, suggestive of the indoor world of women, his womanly form. For this aspect of the god threatens the hard boundaries between categories on which Pentheus insists. But he himself is drawn in complex ways to that womanly condition—both sexually attracted ("you're not impossible to look at") and drawn through identification and longing.

---

[40] On this, see K. J. Dover, *Greek Homosexuality* (Cambridge, Mass., 1978); David Halperin, *One Hundred Years of Homosexuality and Other Essays on Greek Love* (New York, 1990); and John J. Winkler, *The Constraints of Desire: The Anthropology of Sex and Gender in Ancient Greece* (New York, 1990); also M. Foucault, *The Uses of Pleasure*, trans. R. Hurley (New York, 1984).

He desires the condition of womanly passivity, even while he scorns it. He desires the dissolution of boundaries, even while he insists on them most firmly. And the woman's costume in which he delights, deluded, is a revelation and a fulfillment, as well as a disguise. Even as he longs to be cradled in his mother's arms, so he longs more generally for the condition of the female—for a pleasure found in softness, passivity, and the reception of influence—a pleasure altogether forbidden to a free male citizen. The society's depiction of ideal complete maleness as purely active, of passivity as the woman's province, is subverted in complex ways, as we discover that Pentheus' vehement rejection of the female is actually a rejection of a longing deep in himself.

Nor is this merely a point about sexuality narrowly understood. For Pentheus, like most male Athenians of Euripides' time, sees the goal of actively controlling his sexual life as one aspect of a larger project, the project of asserting himself as active, ordering, controlling, rather than as subject to the disorderly and disordering influences of nature. His conflict is not simply between two sexual impulses; it is a more general tension between his desire to fulfill the role of active civilizing leader, maker of order, and his longing for the reception of more turbulent influences, for the voluptuousness of disorder, the darkness of powerlessness. The play's ironic suggestion is that his very attempts to assert himself as keeper of order and embodiment of power deliver him the more surely to disorder and uncontrol.

The play does not present this problem as Pentheus' alone, the result of a personal idiosyncrasy. For it is clear that all citizens must worship Dionysus. Not only the play's contents, but the occasion of its performance at the god's solemn festival, testify to this. It is also clear that this worship gives expression to the longing for pleasure in a certain type of passivity—for the surrender of reason and reason's tight control before the sway of erotic forces and forces of transcendence. In the hands of this god, in the hands of that in him which binds him to the god, each citizen is or becomes feminized, even as each, in actively ordering and choosing, is also masculine. Dionysus himself exemplifies these ambiguities; in expressing his own complex desires, Pentheus reveals his similarity to and kinship with the god. The play's suggestion is, then, that closing off passivity does not avoid passivity, as Athenians might like to believe. It simply brings passivity back in a more pernicious and shameful form. It suggests that any reasonably rich and complete life, sexual or social, is lived in a complex tension between control and yielding, risking always the loss of order. A play about the grim education of a young king, it gives to the young citizens who view it a complex and subversive portrait of the tensions and ambivalences involved in maleness and in leadership, suggesting that neat conventional polarities are inadequate to the complexities of life.

VII

The middle of the cosmos, in the old "simple" picture, was occupied by the human being, a being reasonable and mortal, virtuous and needy, pointing up and down. In the "complex" picture, for example Aristotle's, the human being steps sideways, so to speak, arrogating to itself by itself the place of morality, pity, and compassion, firmly setting itself in opposition both to the serene, uncaring life of the gods and to the dense, uncaring life of the beasts. Aristotle connected this cosmology with his interest in tragedy. For he held that pity and fear, the two emotions most central in an audience's response to tragedy, are emotions connected with this specific and special placement of the human being.[41] Pity, he argues, is an emotion directed at another person's suffering, regarded as both important and undeserved. It requires fellow feeling—that is, the belief that one's own possibilities are similar to those of the sufferer. And what we pity when it happens to another we fear, lest it should happen to us. Fear requires the belief that there are important damages that we may suffer, and that we are powerless to prevent them.[42] Both emotions, then, presuppose that we are needy and not self-sufficient,

[41] See Nussbaum, *Fragility*, Interlude 2; also Stephen Halliwell, *Aristotle's Poetics* and *The Poetics of Aristotle* (both London and Chapel Hill, 1986; the former is an extensive critical discussion, the latter a translation and notes).

[42] See Aristotle, *Rhetoric* 1385b13 ff., *Poetics* 1453a3–5 on pity; *Rhetoric* 1386a22 ff., *Poetics* 1455a4–5 on fear.

not fully in control of the most valuable things. (Both emotions are rejected by thinkers such as Plato and the Stoics, who believe that the good human being *is* entirely self-sufficient for good life, that no big or important reversals can happen beyond people's control.)[43] Both emotions presuppose, too, that human beings are intelligent creatures capable of virtue: for pity makes a firm distinction between what is in our power, and therefore our fault, and what is not, and fear follows pity. Aristotle firmly puts *undeserved*, and therefore pitiable, suffering at the heart of his normative account of tragedy. He himself seems to believe that while the world can damage human life in ways of deep significance, impeding or fostering the active living of a good human life, it cannot produce cruel or evil actions in a good person. Virtue securely holds the human middle ground, and holds the human being *in* that middle ground, preventing egress either up or down.[44]

To a certain extent *The Bacchae* shows a similar understanding of the human middle. And yet Aristotle, in order to accept it fully, would have had to alter his views. The play's final scene between Cadmus and Agave does establish the human world as distinct from both the bestial and the divine. What marks it off is, above all, pity.[45] In the quality of their mutual compassion, in their shared grief over Pentheus' corpse, in their mutual support in the undeserved disasters, Cadmus and Agave distinguish themselves from the god and assert themselves as ethical beings, restoring to their shattered lives a certain wholeness. The dignity of the god is to smile; the dignity of these humans is to weep. The scene in which Pentheus' body is painstakingly reassembled by the pair in grief and pity suggests that it is the capacity for these emotions that is the source of integration

---

[43] Plato, *Republic*, II–III and X; for Stoic views, see the translation and analysis of relevant material in Nussbaum, "The Stoics on the Extirpation of the Passions," *Apeiron* 20 (1987).

[44] Several texts of Aristotle, particularly from the *Rhetoric*, suggest that circumstances can alter character itself (see Nussbaum, *Fragility*, 336–40); but this is not the focus of his discussion in *Nicomachean Ethics I*, where he thinks of character as remaining firm, and focuses on the ways in which circumstances can impede its expression in action: see Nussbaum, *Fragility*, chap. 11.

[45] Cf. also the discussion of pity in Arrowsmith (1959).

and community in human life, the way we piece ourselves together.
Indeed, it suggests as well that human beings, and no one else, are
the sources of whatever integration and community human life pos-
sesses. Enacted in the tragic theater, proverbially a place of pity,
fear, and grief, it suggests to its audience that the tragic festival
itself, and its emotions, are ways of affirming the bonds of a dis-
tinctively human political community, civilized and marked off from
callousness.

All this is Aristotelian. And true, as far as it goes. But I have
said that Aristotle could not approve of, could not accept, this play.
For the human community depicted here is not just subject to sudden
losses and undeserved reversals, the subject matter of pity and grief.
It is subject to stranger changes as well: to sudden ferocity, to blind-
ing insight and searing rage. Virtue's walls are not, as in most of
Aristotle's ethical thought, firm against such incursions. All walls
are to some extent porous, all identities to some extent fluid. Good
character does not, as in Aristotle, stand reliably between the good
person and the possibility of horrible acts. The walls of character,
the ways in which human beings define themselves as orderly and
civilized and good, can themselves shift or give way. And this flu-
idity is not simply weakness; it is, somehow, necessary for a good
and fully human life. Or, to put it differently, the risk we run in
trying to live humanly is not simply a risk of loss; it is a risk of evil.
We do put one another together in pity and in love. But this whole-
ness is human, not bestial, only if it acknowledges Dionysus and so
runs the risk of doing terrible things.[46] Sometimes one may be lucky;
sometimes one murders one's own child; sometimes divine ecstasy
is death.

And this leads to a different view of the tragic theater, one that
we might call trans-Aristotelian: a view in which the theater is not

---

[46] There would be some doubt, however, whether even these deeds are terrible
in Aristotle's sense: for they will not proceed from a stable character trait of a vicious
nature. And *Eudemian Ethics* 1225a20 ff. even suggests that Aristotle might be
prepared to regard them as involuntary, and so deserving of pardon, because produced
by forces that are too strong for human nature to withstand

so much the place where humans set themselves off from the rest of nature, secure in their moral virtue, but the place, instead, where these fluidities and insecurities are enacted, these risks explored.[47] Where, with pity, terror, and a peculiar awe, a community pieces itself together from the fragments of limbs torn in ecstatic rage. Dionysus presides.[48]

Martha Nussbaum
Brown University

BIBLIOGRAPHY

EDITIONS AND COMMENTARIES

Dodds, E. R. (1960). *Euripides, Bacchae: Edited with Introduction and Commentary*. 2nd ed. Oxford.

Kirk, G S. (1970, 1979). *The Bacchae by Euripides: A Translation with Commentary*. Englewood Cliffs, N.J., 1970; repr. as *The Bacchae of Euripides, Translated with an Introduction and Commentary*, Cambridge, England, 1979.

Kopff, E. Christian (1982). *Euripides, Bacchae*. Teubner, Leipzig. (Greek text only.)

Roux, Jeanne (1970 and 1972). *Euripide, Les Bacchantes, I, Introduction, texte et traduction; II, Commentaire*. Paris.

DIONYSUS

Detienne, M. (1979). *Dionysos Slain*. Trans. M. Muellner and L. Muellner. Baltimore and London. Originally published as *Dionysos mis à mort*, Paris, 1977.

——— (1989). *Dionysos at Large*. Trans. A. Goldhammer. Cambridge, Mass. Originally published as *Dionysos à ciel ouvert*, Paris, 1986.

Dodds, E. R. (1940). "Maenadism in the *Bacchae*." *Harvard Theological Review* 33: 155–76. Repr. in part in Dodds (1951), summarized in Dodds (1960), xi–xx.

——— (1951). *The Greeks and the Irrational*. Berkeley and Los Angeles. "The Blessings of Madness," pp. 64–101.

Henrichs, A. (1978). "Greek Maenadism from Olympias to Messalina." *Harvard Studies in Classical Philology* 82: 121–60.

——— (1979). "Greek and Roman Glimpses of Dionysos." In C. Houser, ed. *Dionysos*

---

[47] This conclusion seems consistent with Nietzsche's general view of tragic theater, which—in the case, at least, of this play—seems more adequate to the complexities of the subject than Aristotle's.

[48] I am very grateful to Julia Annas, Jonathan Galassi, Stephen Halliwell, David Konstan, Charles Segal, Zeph Stewart, and C. K. Williams for their extremely helpful comments on an earlier draft of this essay. And I wish to thank Albert Henrichs for his very generous assistance with matters of bibliography.

and His Circle: Ancient Through Modern. Fogg Art Museum, Cambridge, Mass.

———— (1982). "Changing Dionysiac Identities." In B. F. Meyer and E. P. Sanders, eds. *Jewish and Christian Self-Definition III: Self-Definition in the Graeco-Roman World.* London. 137–60 and 213–36.

———— (1984a). "Male Intruders among the Maenads: The So-Called Male Celebrant." In H. D. Evjen, ed. *Mnemai: Classical Studies in Memory of Karl K. Hulley.* Chico, Calif. 69–91.

———— (1984b) "Loss of Self, Suffering, Violence: The Modern View of Dionysus from Nietzsche to Girard." *Harvard Studies in Classical Philology* 88: 205–40.

———— (1987). "Myth Visualized: Dionysos and His Circle in Sixth-Century Attic Vase Painting." In *Papers on the Amasis Painter and His World.* Malibu, Calif. 92–124.

———— (1990). "Between Country and City: Cultic Dimensions of Dionysos in Athens and Attica." In Mark Griffith and D. J. Mastronarde, eds. *Cabinet of the Muses: Studies in Honor of T. G. Rosenmeyer.* Chico, Calif.

Kerényi, K. (1976). *Dionysos: Archetypal Image of Indestructible Life.* Princeton. Originally published as *Dionysos. Urbild des unzerstörbaren Lebens,* Munich and Vienna, 1976.

Nietzsche, F. W. (1872). *The Birth of Tragedy.* Trans. W. Kaufmann. New York, 1976.

Otto, W. (1981). *Dionysus: Myth and Cult.* Bloomington, 1965, repr. Dallas. Originally published as *Dionysos, Mythos und Cultus,* Frankfurt, 1933.

Otto is still the best general introduction. Henrichs's articles provide authoritative detailed accounts of the evidence and the current state of many concrete questions, with wide-ranging references. Detienne's idiosyncratic accounts offer some real insight, but should be used with caution.

STUDIES OF THE PLAY

Arrowsmith, W. (1959). "Introduction to *The Bacchae.*" In D. Grene and R. Lattimore, eds. *The Complete Greek Tragedies. Euripides III* or *V,* depending on the publisher and date.

Arthur, Marylin B (1972). "The Choral Odes of the *Bacchae* of Euripides." *Yale Classical Studies* 22: 145–79.

Burnett, Anne Pippin (1970). "Pentheus and Dionysus: Host and Guest." *Classical Philology* 65: 15–29.

Conacher, D. J. (1967). *Euripidean Drama: Myth, Theme and Structure.* Toronto. 56–77.

Devereux, G. (1970). "The Psychotherapy Scene in Euripides' *Bacchae.*" *Journal of Hellenic Studies* 90: 35–48.

Foley, Helene P. (1985). *Ritual Irony: Poetry and Sacrifice in Euripides.* Ithaca and London. 205–58.

Girard, René (1977). *Violence and the Sacred.* Trans. Patrick Gregory. Baltimore and

London. Chap. V. Originally published as *La Violence et le sacré*, Paris, 1972.

Grube, G. M. A. (1941). *The Drama of Euripides*. London, repr. New York, 1961. 398–420.

Norwood, G. (1908). *The Riddle of the Bacchae*. Manchester, England.

—— (1954). *Essays on Euripidean Drama*. Toronto. 52–73.

Pater, W. (1894). *Greek Studies*. London. Contains "A Study of Dionysus" and "The Bacchanals of Euripides."

Rosenmeyer, T. G. (1968). "Tragedy and Religion: The *Bacchae*." In E. Segal, ed. *Euripides: A Collection of Critical Essays*. Englewood Cliffs, N.J. 150–70. (Essay originally published in Rosenmeyer, *The Masks of Tragedy*, Austin, 1963.)

Sale, W. (1972). "The Psychoanalysis of Pentheus in the *Bacchae* of Euripides." *Yale Classical Studies* 22: 63–83.

—— (1977). *Existentialism and Euripides. Sickness, Tragedy and Divinity in the Medea, the Hippolytus and the Bacchae*. Berwick, Victoria, Australia. 80–123.

Schechner, R. (1969). "In Warm Blood: The *Bacchae*" and "The Politics of Ecstasy." In *Public Domain: Essays on the Theater*. Indianapolis and New York. 93–107, 209–28.

Segal, C. P. (1977) "Euripides' *Bacchae*: Conflict and Mediation." *Ramus* 6: 103–20.

—— (1978). "The Menace of Dionysus: Sex Roles and Reversals in Euripides' *Bacchae*." *Arethusa* 11: 185–202.

—— (1982). *Dionysiac Poetics and Euripides' Bacchae*. Princeton.

—— (1986). "Pentheus and Hippolytus on the Couch and on the Grid: Psychoanalytic and Structuralist Readings of Greek Tragedy" and "Euripides' *Bacchae*: The Language of the Self and the Language of the Mysteries," repr. in Segal. *Interpreting Greek Tragedy: Myth, Poetry, Text*. Ithaca and London. 268–93, 294–312. Also published, respectively, in *Classical World* 72 (1978): 129–48 and in *Die wilde Seele*, Festschrift for George Devereux, ed. Hans Peter Dürr, Frankfurt, forthcoming.

Seidensticker, B. (1979). "Sacrificial Ritual in the *Bacchae*." In G. W. Bowersock, W. Burkert, and M. C. J. Putnam, eds. *Arktouros: Hellenic Studies Presented to B. M. W. Knox*. Berlin and New York. 181–90.

Simon, B. (1978). *Mind and Madness in Ancient Greece: The Classical Roots of Modern Psychiatry*. Ithaca and London.

Verrall, A. W. (1895). *Euripides the Rationalist*. Cambridge, England.

—— (1910). *The Bacchants of Euripides and Other Essays*. Cambridge, England.

Wilamowitz-Moellendorff, U von (1923) *Griechische Tragödien übersetzt*. Vierter Band. Berline. 119–57.

Winnington-Ingram, R. P. (1948). *Euripides and Dionysus: An Interpretation of the Bacchae* Cambridge, England, repr. Amsterdam, 1969.

Translator's Note

Herbert Golder, William Arrowsmith, and Martha Nussbaum all participated at various times in developing this version of *The Bacchae*. None of them is in any sense to be held responsible for what finally appears here, but without their contributions, particularly Professor Golder's, the text would be able to make few claims to accuracy. I would also like to thank Stephen Dobyns, who offered much indispensable help in getting straight matters of tone and diction in the final draft.

The attitude of this translation is that it is just that, a translation, not an imitation or an adaptation. Although I have not tried to account for Greek metrical conventions, feeling that the attempts which have been made to bring quantitatively based poetic forms into English have rarely produced verse of any interest, I have otherwise respected the original as much as possible. No cuts have been made in the text and few liberties have been taken, except for scattered matters of emphasis, particularly in the choruses, and except for one brief moment, oddly enough in the very first lines of the play, about which a few words would seem to be in order. In the Greek, Dionysus' first speech begins with a complex and convoluted sentence: it is almost as though he arrives onstage in the middle of a discourse, a discourse which depends absolutely on his audience knowing who is and assuming a number of things about him, the most evident being that he is a god. In altering those first lines so as to allow Dionysus to iterate some of his many ritual epithets,

I have tried to give him a brief introduction to himself. The few added lines don't, I think, violate at least the tone of the rest of what Dionysus has to say about himself, and given his general frankness and lack of diffidence in such matters it is certainly not out of the range of possibility for him to have made such a self-presentation.

I have made use of various translations: primarily Kirk's, Winnington-Ingram's (as much as he translated in his classic study of the play), and that of the French of Jeanne Roux. There is a gap in the text, beginning in Agave's lament on page 81, after the line that reads, "Father, look at me, how my destiny has turned," and going on into the middle of Dionysus' speech on page 84, where the text picks up again with the line "You will be transfigured into a snake." Some fragments made available to me by Professor Golder allowed me to reconstruct this unfortunate lacuna.

THE CHORUSES

In the version Gregory Dickerson and I published in 1978 of Sophocles' *Women of Trachis* I discussed at some length the theoretical notions which brought me to the system of versification I worked out for the choruses of that play. Since I am using the same method here, it doesn't seem necessary to repeat myself, but I will recapitulate what I have in mind for the performance of the choral odes.

Essentially, my ideas were based on the perception that human beings don't seem to be able to speak in real unison; we can do so only when we have music to order our voices through the abysses of time. "Choral speaking, even at its best," I said in my comments then, "always has something about it of schoolchildren reciting. There is always an imperceptible pause while the group awaits one voice to lead it out of the silence . . . What generally happens is that a kind of sing-song rhythm is generated—the same rhythm that children give to nursery rhymes, and adults to Bible-reading."

Since the music of the Greek tragedies is irrecoverably lost, and since we are reluctant (rightfully so, I believe) to reconstruct or reformulate that music, I felt that perhaps the individual voices of the choruses might be organized by means of the space of the stage, rather than by time.

As I have rendered them, each descending line of each triplet of the choruses (or, as a possible alternative for less experienced actors, each triplet itself) would be spoken by a separate member of the Chorus, so the effect would be that of the actual speeches of the choruses being composed in their passage from one voice to another. There would then be, one would hope, a kind of musicalization of space, and of the language of the odes as they move through that space.

Cast of Characters

DIONYSUS: the son of the god Zeus and the mortal Semele, he was the god of wine, of intoxication, of ecstasy, religious abandon, music, and the ritual hunting and devouring of animals. During Euripides' time, he was still the focus of an active cult. In *The Bacchae* he paradoxically appears both as himself and as the votary of himself, who refers to himself as another while never giving over his own identity. In appearance in the play, he would be quite young, so delicate as to appear almost feminine, with the long, light hair and healthy, flushed cheeks Pentheus so intently remarks.

PENTHEUS (pronounced as two syllables, PEN-theus): the king of Thebes, whose crown has been bestowed on him by his grandfather Cadmus. His mother was Agave, Semele's sister; hence he is the cousin of Dionysus. Another of the sisters was Autonoe, whose son, Actaeon, was turned into a stag by Artemis, and then torn to pieces by his own hounds. For a Greek audience these legends would clearly have added an element of poignancy and tension to Pentheus' dilemma. He is very young, in many of his attitudes still an adolescent, with an adolescent's fascinations and fears. At the same time, he is indeed a king; he feels the responsibilities of a king and has an imperious sense of power and propriety.

CADMUS: the grandfather of Pentheus, and of Dionysus. He is very old now, doddering, but in his prime was the founder of Thebes. In

Greek tradition, he had constant doings with divinity and myth. Among the most crucial of these, in terms of this play, was his slaying of a dragon and the sowing of its teeth, from which warriors miraculously came forth, the best of whom composed the army he used to establish his city. (Hence the references in the play to the "sown men.") He married Harmonia, the daughter of the god Ares and the goddess Aphrodite.

TIRESIAS: the blind seer. He was an important figure in Greek myth, with various astonishing attributes, including his having become a woman for a time, but in Euripides' version, he, too, is very old, as well as rather banal, a kind of sophist, pompous, pedantic, conservative.

AGAVE: Pentheus' mother, the daughter of Cadmus. She, with her surviving sisters, Autonoe and Ino, are among the women who have fled Thebes, and each leads her own band of Maenads.

THE CHORUS: the adepts of Dionysus, who have followed him from Asia, and who are thus strangers in Thebes. They are the Bacchae, also known as Bacchants, or Maenads, who are entirely dedicated to the ecstatic worship of the god. The women of Thebes, too, have become Bacchants, but against their will, driven to madness and out of their homes to wander on the mountain Cithaeron, where Dionysus reigns and where his rituals are enacted. The costume of the Bacchae is described in the course of the play, but a word should be said about the "thyrsus," which is mentioned again and again. The thyrsus was a rod, a wand, of fennel, with ivy bound to it. It played an important part in the Bacchae's dances, and symbolically was closely associated with them, being, in fact, almost their insignia.

There are two messengers, one a cowherd, one who goes with Pentheus on his journey to Cithaeron, and a guard.

THE BACCHAE

of Euripides

The royal palace of Thebes.
To one side, a tomb covered with vines, and the rubble of a house, with
smoke rising from it.

Enter Dionysus

DIONYSUS

I am Dionysus. I am Bacchus.
Bromius and Iacchus.
Dithyrambus and Evius.
I am a god, the son of Zeus,
but I have assumed the semblance of a mortal,
and come to Thebes, where my mother, Semele,
the daughter of King Cadmus, gave birth to me.
Her midwife was the lightning bolt that killed her.
There is the river Dirce, and there the stream
Ismenus. Over there, near the palace,
is my mother's tomb, and her ruined house,
still smoldering with the living flame of Zeus,
Hera's unrelenting hatred towards her.
I praise Cadmus. He made the ruins hallowed ground,
dedicated to his daughter. I myself
caused these vines to grow so thickly on them.

I was in Phrygia before I came here,
and Lydia, where the earth flows gold. I passed
the broiling plains of Persia, and Bactria's

walled towns. The Medes then, their freezing winters,
then opulent Arabia and down
along the bitter, salt-sea coast of Asia
where Hellenes and barbarians mingle
in teeming, beautifully towered cities.
When I had taught my dances there, established
the rituals of my mystery, making
my divinity manifest to mortals,
I came to Greece, to Thebes, the first Greek city
I've caused to shriek in ecstasy for me,
the first whose women I've clothed in fawnskin and in
whose hands I've placed my ivy spear, the thyrsus.
Why did I choose Thebes? Because my mother's sisters,
who should have been the last to even *think*
of saying such a thing, started rumors:
that Dionysus was *not* the son of Zeus,
that Semele's lover had been a mortal
and she'd imputed the disgrace to Zeus, a fraud
Cadmus had contrived. They kept whispering
that Zeus destroyed her because she'd lied and said
he was her lover. Therefore I've stung them
with madness, and goaded them raving from their houses.
They're living on the mountain now, delirious,
dressed, as I've compelled them to be dressed,
in the garments of my rituals.
And all the rest, the whole female seed of Thebes,
I've driven frenzied out of house and home.
They're with the daughters of King Cadmus now,
huddled on bare rocks beneath the pines.
This city must learn, and know, against its will or not,
that it is uninitiated in my mysteries.
As for Semele, her memory
will be vindicated when I appear
to mortal eyes as the power she bore Zeus.
Cadmus has abdicated now to Pentheus,

the son of Agave, another of his daughters,
and Pentheus is warring with divinity
by excluding me from rituals
and not invoking my name in prayers.

Because of this, I'm going to demonstrate to him
and to all Thebes the god I really am.
When order is established, I'll go on,
revealing my identity in other lands.
But if, by rage and force of arms, the citizens
of Thebes drive the Bacchae from the mountain,
then I lead the army of my Maenads into war.
This is why I have assumed a mortal shape,
shedding my divine form for a human's.

Dionysus calls to the Chorus.

Now, women, come: all you who left the ramparts
of Tmolus, who left Lydia, left barbarian lands
to follow me and worship me, my women: come.
Bring the drum we brought from Phrygia,
the drum that pulses with the beat of Mother Earth.
Surround the royal walls of Pentheus with thunder:
let the city of King Cadmus see!

I am going to the gorges of Cithaeron now;
I am going to the Bacchae, to their dances.

Enter Chorus.

Exit Dionysus.

CHORUS*
  Down
   from Asia, down
    from sacred Tmolus

* See "The Choruses" in "Translator's Note."

I have soared and
  soar, still, for
    Bromius, in
the labor, difficult,
  difficult
    and sweet, the
sweet, exacting labor
  of exalting
    him, of crying
out
    for him, *Bacchus,*
    holy Bacchus!

Who is in
  the road,
    who
is in
  the
    streets and who
is in
  the palace, in
    its chambers?
Be here,
  now, be
    here, anyone,
anywhere, be
  here, lips
    dedicated,
pious, purified, be
  here, now, as
    I, as all, all
sing the
  ancient
    blessings, the
ancient, hallowed

blessings
  of Dionysus!

Blessed, blessed
  and happy,
    blessed and
blessed again
  are they who,
    in the holy
rituals,
  consecrate themselves,
    who
know the
  mysteries.
    Blessed
in spirit, blessed
  spirit fused,
    fused
with and consecrated
  to the holy
    bands upon
the mountains,
  the bands
    of Bacchus praying
in the mountains,
  blessing, praising
    Bacchus, holy
Bacchus,
  blessed
    with purity and
blessed
  with prayer. And
    the rituals
of our great mother
  Cybele, and

the rituals
of the ivy-covered
thyrsus and the ritual
of its rattling,
of the rattling of
the ivy of
the holy wand,
holy
thyrsus, and
the ritual
of the holy, ivy-
covered crown of
Bacchus.

Plummet
down, now,
Bacchants, plummet
down,
hover,
Bacchants, down,
down from
Phrygia, down
its mountains,
down
to here, the
broad
ways here, lead
Bromius down,
Bromius,
Dionysus, god, son
of god and
god, lead
him down!
Bromius! Roarer!
Roarer!

Once, she,
  his
    mother, of
whom, in
  agony, and in
    a blast
of fire from
  Zeus, he
    was born;
once,
  his mother, from
    whom he
was torn out
  by Zeus's lightning . . .
    And
she died with
  it, and he,
    then,
by his father,
  Zeus, son
    of Cronos,
was caught,
  uplifted, and,
    that
instant, pinned,
  with golden
    clips,
into his holy
  thigh, and
    he kept
him there, a
  secret
    from his wife,
a gold-
  bound secret

from Hera,
wife of
Zeus . . .
And it was
Zeus who,
when the
time
the fates deemed
proper
came,
it was
Zeus who
brought him
forth again, to
his birth
again,
a god,
though, now,
horned,
horns rising
like
a bull's
now, horns
flourished, garlanded
with
beast-nourished
serpents, and
his Maenads,
too, in their
tresses, too,
weave
serpents, all
his holy
Maenads.
Thebes, O

Thebes, who nurtured
   her, Semele,
garland now
   yourself, Thebes, with
     ivy garlands
now and
   with myrtle, luscious
     myrtle, crown
yourself and
   with oak and
     fir-twigs; be the
Bacchant now,
   yourself, and
     dappled fawnskins
wrap
   upon yourself,
     and
white curls of
   braided wool,
     take unto
yourself the wild
   thyrsus now,
     behold, now,
yourself, behold,
   holy now,
     all the land,
yourself and all
   the land, shall
     dance now,
dance
   again, when
     Bromius leads
the dance
   onto the
     holy

mountain!
  Bromius
    calls
his band and
  leads them
    where, already,
one band
  waits, the band
    of women
waits, driven
  from their
    looms, driven
from
  their shuttles,
    stung,
stung by
  Dionysus, from
    themselves!

Oh, and
  you, the
    holy
caves of
  Crete, the
    dens
of the Curetes,
  the
    caves where
Zeus was
  born and where
    the drum,
too, was
  born, was given
    by you, you
who wear

three helmets,
   you,
Corybants, you
  who made my
    leather drum for
me and
  danced for
   me, and who,
dancing out
  the Bacchic rites,
   mixed
the drumbeat
  into the wild,
    ecstatic dances
with the sharp,
  sweet calling
   crying
of the flute, and
  handed
   it, my
drum, to her, Mother
  Rhea, so
   that she
could hand it
  to the Satyrs, who
   were wild with
dancing, too,
  and
   brought
it to the dances
  now
   in which
Dionysus, in
  his gigantic
   year, in

his festival
  exults—
    Holy Dionysus!

Delectable he
  is, delectable,
    upon
the mountain and he
  falls out of
    the holy bands, onto
the ground; delectable
  he is, in the
    holy
fawnskin, and he
  joyfully
    devours the living
flesh of new-
  ly slaughtered goats and
    on the mountain
now, again,
  in Phrygia,
    in Lydia, and
always, rushing
  everywhere
    before
us, sweetly calling,
  is
    Bromius!
And the earth
  flows, flows
    beneath us, then
milk
  flows, and wine
    flows,
and nectar

flows, like
  flame,
like the fire
  from Syria, from
    the frankincense,
delectable, the
  flame that
    flows, now,
from
  his torch, and rushes,
    flowing now,
from his thyrsus
  as he whirls
    it, runs
with it, rushes,
  driving on his
    dancers with
it, roaring
  on
    with it, and
his locks
  flow thickly and
    his locks dance
and *Onwards,*
  Bacchae, he
    is roaring, *Onwards,*
Bacchae,
  blazing with
    the gold of
golden Tmolus,
  Evohe! he
    roars, *Evohe!* he
calls, *Sing*
  to Dionysus,
    Sing!

And make
  the drums, make
    the
drums
  roar, let the drums
    honor
Bacchus, let
  the flute shriek, and
    the holy
shriekings
  are delectable and
    holy and now
shriek again, it
  is woven
    now, together,
the holy flute,
  the way up
    to the
mountain,
  holiness and
    mountain!
And the
  Bacchant
    then, as
joyful
  as a foal
    near
its mother,
  grazing, leaps,
    cavorts,
prances, so
  she dances
    now,
the Bacchant,
  and she

                        soars
                  now, being,
                        now,
                          joy-
                  fully, playfully,
                        the
                          Bacchant.

Enter Tiresias.

TIRESIAS

Who is at the gates? Call Cadmus from the house:
the son of Agenor, who came from Sidon
to build the walls and towers of Thebes.
Tell him Tiresias is here. He'll know why.
He and I, ancient and more ancient, have made vows:
to adorn ourselves with fawnskins, with Bacchic wands,
and to wreathe shoots of ivy in our hair.

Enter Cadmus.

CADMUS

I knew it was you, old friend. I was in the palace,
but I recognized that wise old voice of yours.
You always know a voice like that, the wisdom in it.
Here I am, in the god's equipment, all prepared.
He's my daughter's son. We have to lift him high,
as high as possible—Dionysus,
who's revealed himself to mortals as a god.
Now, where will the dancing be? Show me
where my feet should go: they'll dance; we'll toss
these old white manes of ours. Explain where,
Tiresias, old man to old man: you're wise.
I'll dance all day and night and not get tired,
beating my thyrsus on the ground. In our joy,
we've even forgotten how we've gotten on.

TIRESIAS

That's it, that's how I feel, young, too.
I'll dance, I'll take my chances.

CADMUS

Shall we ride in a chariot to the mountain?

TIRESIAS

No, we'll walk, it will show more reverence.

CADMUS

We're both old, but shall I lead you?

TIRESIAS

The god will lead us without our trying.

CADMUS

Are we the only men who'll dance for Dionysus?

TIRESIAS

Only we can see. The rest of them are mad.

CADMUS

Let's not waste time. Let me lead you there.

TIRESIAS

Here, take my hand in yours.

CADMUS

I'm only human: I won't despise the gods.

TIRESIAS

Compared with their wisdom, ours is nothing.
What comes down to us, from our fathers,
out of ancient time, no argument's more powerful
than that: the wisest mind can't theorize past that.
When I put on my ivy now, and go to dance,
they'll say, "Old fool, shameless fool,"
but the god makes no distinction, old or young:
he wants us all to honor him, he wants
us united in his exaltation.

CADMUS

Since you can't see this sight, Tiresias,
let me tell you what's about to happen.
Pentheus, the son of Echion,

to whom I've resigned my powers as king,
is rushing towards the palace. He seems agitated.

Enter Pentheus.

PENTHEUS

I happened to be gone from Thebes, now I hear
awful evils have erupted in the city.
Our women have deserted home to perpetrate
false Bacchic mysteries in the dark woods
on the mountain, dancing to celebrate their upstart
deity, Dionysus . . . whoever Dionysus is.
They fill great bowls of wine, then they creep
into the bushes and lie down for lusting men.
Priestesses, they say they are, Maenads,
sworn to Bacchus. I say if it's anyone
they're dedicated to, it's Aphrodite.
Some of them I've had trapped: they're in prison,
chained. The rest are in the hills.
I'll track them down, all of them, even Agave,
my mother, and her sisters, Ino,
and Autonoe, the mother of Actaeon.
I'll have them all in cages.
I'll stamp out these obscene orgies.
There's an intruder, too, I hear, a foreigner,
a sorcerer, a charlatan, from Lydia.
Long, scented yellow hair, they say, cheeks like wine,
with Aphrodite's love charms in his eyes.
Day and night he mixes with young girls,
holding his mysteries up for them to admire.
Once I get him here, though, inside the walls,
he won't be tossing his locks or beating the ground
with his famous thyrsus. Not when I have his head.
He's the one who claims Dionysus is a god,
that he was stitched into the thigh of Zeus,
when really the child and the mother were both

consumed by lightning, because she'd lied
and said that Zeus had been her lover.
I don't know who this stranger is,
but doesn't such insulting outrage deserve hanging?

He sees Cadmus and Tiresias.

Not another miracle! Look: the seer,
rigged up in dappled fawnskin—Tiresias himself.
And my mother's father, you, too, decked out
like a Bacchant with your thyrsus. Ridiculous!
Are you both senile? I'm ashamed, Grandfather.
Shake that ivy off, right away;
let go of that thyrsus. Tiresias,
you instigated this! One more imported deity,
more flocks of birds for you to read,
more burnt offerings to get fees for!
You're fortunate you're old, that's why
you're not shackled with the Bacchae
for having brought these wretched rites to Thebes.
Whenever wine gleams at a women's feast,
I say nothing's healthy in those mysteries.

CHORUS LEADER

This is impiety! Stranger, do you offer reverence
neither to the gods, nor to Cadmus,
who sowed the crop of those born of the earth?
You, the son of Echion, will you deny your race?

TIRESIAS

If a wise man finds an honest case to argue,
being eloquent is hardly difficult.
As for you, though your glibness gives you the air
of being sane, there's nothing rational about you.
A man who influences others with overbearing
is dangerous for his city: he lacks reason.
This new god you're subjecting to ridicule,
I can't tell you how great he'll be

throughout Greece.
There are, young man,
two principles for humankind: first, the goddess
Demeter—you can call her that, or Earth—
who nourishes us with solid food. Then comes
the son of Semele, equal in power, who invented
and introduced to mortals the liquid of the grape,
which gives weak humans surcease from pain,
when they're glutted with the liquor of the vine,
and gives us sleep, to forget the evils of our days.
There is no other remedy for our affliction.
He, a god himself, is poured as a libation to the gods,
it's thanks to him men have these blessings.

You sneer at him being sewn into the thigh
of Zeus? I'll teach you what that really means.
When Zeus snatched the newborn from the lightning
and carried him up onto Olympus as a god,
Hera wanted to throw the child from heaven,
but Zeus, in his godly wisdom, countered her.
Breaking off a fragment of the ether
the world floats in, he made a doll, a Dionysus-
doll, that he showed Hera. But men confused
the words: they garbled "showed" to "sewed" and made
the story up about his having "sewed"
the god in his thigh to hide him from Hera.

And this god is a prophet, too: the Bacchic
frenzy gives the power of foresight; when
Bacchus fully infiltrates the body
of whoever is possessed, they foretell the future.
Dionysus even has a share
of the god of war: an army will be ranged
with arms for battle—before a lance is lifted,
a panic suddenly takes them and they flee.
This dementia also comes from Dionysus.

Someday you'll see him soaring on the rocks
at Delphi, leaping with pine torches
on the double cliffs, his Bacchic thyrsus
whirling, lashing, great in all Greece.
Pentheus, listen: don't believe that power
dominates in human life, and though
your sick imagination makes you think it,
don't believe you're sane. Welcome the god,
offer him libations, be a Bacchant, wear garlands.
It's not Dionysus who'll compel
a woman to be virtuous: chastity
is a part of one's nature or it's not;
even plunged in the deliriums of ritual,
a woman who is truly chaste won't be corrupted.

You know you're proud when your name is glorified,
when the multitude cries "Pentheus!" from the towers.
I believe the god is pleased by homage, too.
Therefore both Cadmus and I, the butt of your jokes,
will wreathe our heads with ivy and we'll dance:
gray-haired or not, both of us will dance.
You won't persuade me to fight the god.
You're mad, and there are no drugs to heal you,
because you must be drugged to be this painfully mad.

CHORUS LEADER

Old man, Apollo would approve your words.
Honoring the great god Bromius proves your wisdom.

CADMUS

My boy, the advice Tiresias is offering is good.
Believe him. Live with us. Don't break tradition.
For the moment, you're distracted, deluded.
But besides, even if the god isn't a god,
say he is: it's a pious lie. Semele,
the mother of a god: consider the honor
it brings our family and remember Actaeon:
his death, how horrible it was; the hounds

he'd raised with meat from his own hands,
tearing him to pieces on the mountain,
because he bragged he could outhunt Artemis.
Don't let that be you. Here, I'll crown you
with ivy: stay with us, offer homage to the god.

PENTHEUS

Don't touch me! Go play with your Bacchus,
but don't wipe your madness off on me.
And Tiresias, the instructor of your foolishness,
will pay for this.

Enter guards.

Someone, quickly, go,
now, to the place where he observes his birds.
Take a lever, turn the whole thing over, demolish it,
throw his sacred garlands to the storming winds.
There's no way I can hurt him more than that.
The rest of you, patrol the city.
That girlish stranger who's introduced this new plague
and fouled our beds—I want him. Track him down
and when you find him, tie him up, bring him here,
so he can get what he deserves, death by stoning.
He'll rue the Bacchic orgies he'll find in Thebes.

Exit guards.

TIRESIAS

You poor fool. You don't know the meaning
of your own words. Before, you were insane,
now you're raving. Come, Cadmus, we'll pray for him.
May the god have pity on the wild man and may
he not inflict reprisals on the city.
Come, we'll support one another.
Hold your thyrsus. Two old men,
we mustn't fall, we would be disgraced.
We must serve Bacchus, son of Zeus, and so we will.
Cadmus, beware that Pentheus doesn't make your house

repent. This isn't prophecy, but fact:
the fool speaks foolishness.

Exit Pentheus to the palace. Exit Cadmus and Tiresias to Cithaeron.

CHORUS
Holiness, queen
     of all the
          gods, Holiness,
who to
     the earth
          hovers
down, on
     gold
          wings, down
to us: do
     you hear
          him? Do you
hear this
     Pentheus, his
          unholy,
raging insolence
     against the
          god? Against
Bromius, son of
     Semele, most
          blessed, most
holy, of the
     divine, who,
          at the god's
lovely garlanded
     celebration, has
          this gift, to
dance, to bring men,
     to bring men
          together in
the dance, and

this,
    when the
flute shrieks, to
    laugh, and
        this, to
stop cares, to
    stop
        woe, and
when the glistening
    wine
        into the holy,
ivy-bearing
    god-feast comes,
        to banish
everything, to wrap
    us all
        in sleep.

Tongues
    without bits;
        defiance
without law:
    together
        they create
disaster.
    But this, the
        life
of calm, the
    life of rational
        tranquillity, this
sustains us, this
    holds our house
        together.

The gods
    are far from

us: how far
in their azure
  are they, how
  far they
are, in their
  eons: but still
  they
watch us,
  see us, see
    our actions,
watch
  our
    goings on.

Knowledge
  is not wisdom:
    cleverness
is not, not
  without
    awareness
of our
  death,
    not
without recalling
  just how
    brief
our flare
  is. He
    who overreaches
will, in his
  overreaching, lose
    what
he possesses,
  betray
    what

he has
   now. That
      which is
beyond us,
   which is
      greater
than
   the human, the
      unattainably
great, is
   for
      the mad, or
for those
   who listen
      to
the mad, and then
   believe
      them.

Oh, let me, let
   me go, let
      me go
to Cyprus,
   Aphrodite's
      island, where
the heart's
   beguilers,
      tempters
of men's
   hearts
      live.

Oh, there, at
   Paphos,
      where, with

no rain,
    the river
        with a hundred
mouths
    brings forth gigantic
        harvests.
There, or
    Pieria, lovely
        Pieria, where
Olympus
    is, where
        the muses
have their holy
    place; take me
        there,
Master, O
    Bromius, there
        the Graces
are, there
    Desire, and there
        the Bacchants
can lawfully
    enact their holy
        rites.
The god, the
    son of
        Zeus, finds
rituals
    joyful! He
        cherishes
peace, and peace
    cherishes
        the
young. He
    brings goodness to

both
rich and
  lesser mortals,
    offering
all, all
  happiness, all
    wine,
all
  painlessness
    and pleasure.
They, though,
  who
    will not take
these
  gifts, who
    refuse
the happiness of
  those
    who choose to
live a life
  rich by
    day and
blessed at night, those
  he detests! He
    detests excess,
detests
  insatiable, excessive
    men!
And so, what
  the common man
    thinks, what
the simple
  man believes, the
    most
humble, that

I, too,

will

take

as my

example.

Enter guards, leading Dionysus, bound. Enter Pentheus.

GUARD

Pentheus, here we are: we've hunted down
the prey you wanted. Except . . .
the animal was tame: he didn't try to run,
he never lost the flushed wine color in his cheeks.
He just smiled, gave us his hands, told us
we'd better tie him. I felt ashamed. "Stranger,"
I said, "I'm doing this against my will:
it's Pentheus who gave the order."
And those women you had chained, locked
in the dungeon? Well, they're gone now.
They're off in the meadows, dancing,
calling on their god Bromius. The chains around
their legs just snapped, the barred doors
came open by themselves: no mortal did all that.
This person who's come to Thebes is full of miracles.
But all this is your responsibility.

PENTHEUS

Untie his hands, he's in my net,
he won't be dancing out of this.
Well, you're not impossible to look at, are you?
Women wouldn't think so, anyway. Not in Thebes,
they wouldn't, which is why you're here, of course.
What a mane of hair you have: very seductive.
Look at it falling down your cheeks.
Good hand holds for a wrestler.
And how white your skin is: you must be careful
about staying out of the sun.

Oh, yes, handsome you, in the shade,
hunting with Aphrodite. All right, who are you?

DIONYSUS

I'll tell you, I have no secrets.
You've heard of Tmolus of the thousand flowers?

PENTHEUS

I know it, it flanks the town of Sardis.

DIONYSUS

I come from there, my country is Lydia.

PENTHEUS

Why have you brought these rituals to Greece?

DIONYSUS

By command of Dionysus, son of Zeus.

PENTHEUS

Is there a Zeus in Lydia spawning new gods?

DIONYSUS

No, it's your Zeus, who married Semele.

PENTHEUS

He commanded you . . . Face to face, or in a dream?

DIONYSUS

He revealed his mysteries face to face.

PENTHEUS

And these mysteries: what are they?

DIONYSUS

They are forbidden, unutterable to unbelievers.

PENTHEUS

What do they confer on those who sacrifice?

DIONYSUS

It would be sacrilege to tell, but there's great good.

PENTHEUS

You're clever. You want to make me curious.

DIONYSUS

The mysteries detest an impious man.

PENTHEUS

You say you saw the god: what form did he take?

DIONYSUS

Any form he wanted to—it wasn't my doing.

PENTHEUS

Another evasion. You make no sense.

DIONYSUS

Sense *is* nonsense, for a fool.

PENTHEUS

Is Thebes the first stop on your god's itinerary?

DIONYSUS

No, foreigners everywhere dance to him.

PENTHEUS

Foreigners are less intelligent than Greeks.

DIONYSUS

In this, more intelligent: customs vary.

PENTHEUS

Do you perform your mysteries by day, or at night?

DIONYSUS

Usually at night: there's more awe in darkness.

PENTHEUS

And for women, more treachery and corruption.

DIONYSUS

There's corruption in broad daylight, too.

PENTHEUS

Cheap sophistries! You'll pay for them.

DIONYSUS

You'll pay, for your impiety and stubbornness.

PENTHEUS

Well, Bacchic backtalk. You wrestle well, with words.

DIONYSUS

Tell me, how do you propose to punish me?

PENTHEUS

First I'll shear those lovely locks of yours.

DIONYSUS

My hair is holy: I've grown it for the god.

PENTHEUS

Now your thyrsus, you'll hand that over.

DIONYSUS

You'll have to take it: it belongs to Dionysus.

PENTHEUS

Now I'll put you in chains, in prison.

DIONYSUS

The god will free me, when I want him to.

PENTHEUS

Call him all you like, you and your Bacchae.

DIONYSUS

He's here now, seeing what I'm suffering.

PENTHEUS

Where is he? I don't see anything.

DIONYSUS

He's with me. You're unholy. You can't see.

PENTHEUS

Tie him up! He's scorning Thebes and me!

DIONYSUS

I am sane. I won't be bound by the insane.

PENTHEUS

I say bind him! I'm the power here, not you!

DIONYSUS

Your power is mortal, you don't know what
you're doing: you don't even know who you are.

PENTHEUS

I am Pentheus. Son of Echion. Son of Agave.

DIONYSUS

Pentheus, Pentheus, you'll repent that name.

PENTHEUS

Take him. Lock him up. Put him in the stable.
If it's dark he wants, give him darkness.
Go dance there. And your women,
your accomplices, I'll sell them as slaves,
or keep them in my house, laboring at looms,
instead of beating on their maddening drums.

DIONYSUS

Take me. What isn't to be suffered won't be.

But you: Dionysus, whom you've offered outrage to,
whose very being you deny, will punish you.
Wrong us, it's him you bind in chains.

The guards lead Dionysus off. Pentheus follows.

CHORUS

Queen
  Dirce, you are
    the daughter
of Achelous;
  holy
    Dirce, more
than holy, for
  to you Zeus
    once
touched his
  child, touched him
    to your waters
as he tore
  him from the unrelenting
    fire
and placed him
  in his thigh and
    roared:
You
  are Dithyrambus!
    Into my male
womb, come!
  You
    are Bacchus!
Come, I will
  reveal you to
    Thebes!
You
  are Bacchus!

They
shall call
   you
     Bacchus!
But you, Dirce,
  blessed
    river, you
thrust me from
  you, you thrust the
    garlanded
bands who dance
  near you. Why
    thrust me from
you this way? Why
  shun me
    so? Soon,
though, by
  the luscious grapes
    of Dionysus'
vines, I swear
  soon the name
    Bromius
will have
  a meaning for
    you, too.

Rage, and
  rage and rage
    is what
he, this
  earth-child,
    this
Pentheus,
  dragon's
    seed, this

monstrous
  son
    of Echion,
reveals, an earth-
  child, just
    as the monstrous
giants are,
  children of
    the earth, as
they, gory, wild-
  faced, rage, so
    he, daring,
daring to dare
  gods, rages, and
    will
dare, soon,
  too, to
    threaten
me, with
  chains, and who
    already, in
his house, in
  the darkness of
    his prison,
has
  my dancing
    comrade.

Do
  you see us?
    Do you
see these
  things, son
    of Zeus?
Dionysus,

do you see
   our battle,
our suffering
   in
      oppression?
Come, be
   with us, come
      down from
Olympus,
   come whirl
      your thyrsus with
its golden
   face
      quell
this vile person's
   insolence
      and violence!

Are you on
   Nysa now, which
      nurtures
beasts, or are
   you now,
      Dionysus,
guiding with your
   wand bands
      of dancers in
the mountains of
   Corycia?
      Or on
Olympus, in
   the forest
      where
Orpheus played
   his lyre and brought,

with his
muse, the
trees
to him and
the ferocious
beasts to
him, are
you there? Oh,
Pieria,
blessed,
honors you and with
your own cries,
Evius, honors
you, and he
will come
dance
in Bacchic
celebrations, and
over the
roaring river
Axios will
spin
his Maenads, and
over the
rich
waters of
Lydias
spin them,
Lydias,
bliss-giver,
father, whose lovely
waters make that
land of horses
gleam.

Dionysus' voice is heard from offstage.

DIONYSUS

Listen!
Listen to me, Bacchae!
I am calling! Listen, Bacchae, listen to me!

CHORUS

Who? To
whom
listen?
Whose
call? Whose
call, O
Evius, where
are you to listen
to, Evius?

DIONYSUS

Again! Listen! I call again!
The son of Zeus, the son of Semele, calls again!

CHORUS

Bromius!
Roarer!
You!
Lord! You
come to us, oh,
be here, lord!

DIONYSUS

Earthquake! Be here! Shake the world!
Come, shudder the foundations of the world!

CHORUS

Look, the
palace, Pentheus,
his palace, look,
it shudders, the
whole palace trembles, now
it falls!
Dionysus!
Look! Dionysus!

Loved one!
Dionysus now is in
the palace! Love him,
oh, we adore
him! Look, the lintels
craze, and
look, the stones
craze! Over
the pillars, crazing,
the stone shatters!
Listen, now: Bromius!
Bromius roars! He roars
now, Bromius!

DIONYSUS

Roar, lightning! Roar, bolt! Fire!
Let the fire consume! Consume and roar!

CHORUS

Look!
The fire, look,
it roars
upon
the tomb
of Semele! Look!
The fire-
bolt, Zeus's
fire,
it falls upon
the fire of
Semele!
Fall,
Maenads!
Fall!
There, the
ground, fall
to it!

Tremble! Look!
  Our lord, the
    son
of Zeus, has
  brought these
    high
halls
  down to
    ruin.

Enter Dionysus.

DIONYSUS

Ah, my Oriental women: did you fall?
Why? Was it fear that made you fall?
You saw the house of Pentheus, when Dionysus
made it shake, and you were shaken, too, by fear.
Come, no fear now, no fall: rise.

CHORUS LEADER

O Light, without you there was no dance,
I was lost without you, Light.

DIONYSUS

Were you lost when I was locked in there?
In the dark there, in the net of Pentheus?
Did you think that I was lost?

CHORUS LEADER

I was lost. What else, without you, but lost?
The man who has no god had you. How are you free?

DIONYSUS

I saved myself. It took no effort.

CHORUS LEADER

But he'd bound your hands in knots!

DIONYSUS

That was how I took my vengeance on him,
how I humiliated him: he tried to bind me,

his hands, though, never touched me;
he fed on his desires. A bull was in there,
by its stall—my jail, he thought. He took his ropes
and bent to wind them on its knees and hooves.
He was panting: *rage!* He was sweating, dripping,
biting at his lips. I was right there next to him.
I watched him. I was quiet. Then Bromius
revealed himself. The house shook! The grave
of Semele shot flames! Pentheus cried out.
He thought the palace was in flames.
Where are all my slaves? he cried. He ran.
The slaves ran. *Water!* he shouted, *from the river,
from Achelous*, but all their work was futile.
Then he stopped. He thought of me: I might escape.
He drew a pitch-black sword and ran into the palace.
But it seems Bromius must have made a shape,
in the courtyard: Pentheus stabbed at it,
at the gleaming air, as though it were me.
Bacchus wasn't finished, though, humiliating him.
The palace crashes down, everything is shattered.
Now Pentheus can see the bitterness my chains
have brought him. His sword falls. He's exhausted.
A man, a mortal, dares to struggle with a god!
I left him there. I walked out quietly to you.
Pentheus! What is he to me? I imagine he'll be coming.
Listen to him tramping through the courtyard.
I'll be patient: let him rage. Wise men
know how to practice self-control.

Enter Pentheus and guards.

PENTHEUS

Terrible: that stranger, that man I had in chains . . .
he's escaped . . . *You!*
What are you doing here, at the gate?
How did you get out?

DIONYSUS

Step calmly with your anger.

PENTHEUS

How did you escape your bonds?

DIONYSUS

Weren't you listening when I told you
someone would be here to free me?

PENTHEUS

Someone? You keep making riddles.

DIONYSUS

Someone who makes grapevines grow for human beings.

PENTHEUS

The gift of wine! You reproach this god yourself!
I want the tower gates all closed.

DIONYSUS

Can't gods leap over walls?

PENTHEUS

You're very wise. Except when you should be wise.

DIONYSUS

Wisest of all when I have to be.
Wait, though, someone's running towards us.
He's coming from the mountain with a message.
We'll wait, we won't try to run away.

Enter Messenger.

MESSENGER

Pentheus. King of Thebes.
I come from Cithaeron,
where the white snow gleams
and falls and never falters . . .

PENTHEUS

Is this news urgent?

MESSENGER

I've seen the holy Bacchae, the women from Thebes,
who shot bare-legged out of the city like arrows.

I want to tell it to you, lord,
to the entire city. It's astonishing,
a miracle . . . May I speak freely, though?
You have a temper, lord. I'm afraid
of you, of your royal rage.

PENTHEUS

Speak, I won't hurt you. Tell me everything.
Being angry with an honest man is wrong.
The more scandalous the things you tell about
the Bacchae, though, the more the man who gave
the women those ideas is going to suffer.

MESSENGER

Our cattle were just coming up
the last ridge to the high meadow.
The sun was barely in the sky,
just starting to warm the ground,
when I saw them, the dancers, all three
troops of them, with their leaders.
Autonoe first, then Agave, your mother,
and finally, Ino.
All of them were sound asleep, some
stretched out on pine boughs,
others lying modestly here and there
among the oak leaves, their heads on the ground.
They were drunk with wine, but not
the way you say, intoxicated with shrieking
flutes and driven into ecstasies
tracking Aphrodite in the bushes.
But then your mother, hearing
the lowing of our stock, was on her feet,
letting out a ritual scream, and then
the rest of the Bacchae, in one bound,
as though with a single mind, woke,
too, rubbing their eyes like children.
There were old women and young,

and unmarried girls: all wonderfully
well disciplined. They shook their long hair
out over their shoulders. The ones whose
fawnskin robes had slipped refastened them
with living snakes, whose tongues
flickered over the women's cheeks.
I saw mothers who'd abandoned babies;
their breasts gorged with milk, they held
wolf cubs in their arms, or young
gazelles, and were suckling them.
Now they all put garlands on their heads,
flowering myrtle and oak leaves.
Now one, with her thyrsus, strikes
a rock: living water fountains up.
Another drives her wand into the ground:
the god jets up a spring of wine.
If they wanted milk to drink,
they scratched at the earth with their nails
and milk streamed for them, and pure honey
spurted from the tips of their wands.
If you had been there, sire,
if you had seen these miracles,
believe me, the god whom you abuse now
you'd supplicate with prayers.

We, the shepherds and cow-tenders,
all of us there watching, were all
talking at once by then, trying
to explain to one another the wonderful
and awful things they were doing.
Then someone, a wanderer, who'd spent
time in town and had a way
with words, said to us: "Listen,
all of you who live up here
on the holy highlands

of the mountains, don't you want
to curry favor with the king?
Let's hunt down Agave for him
and drag her from those dances."
We let him talk us into it.
We set up ambush in the brush,
camouflaged with leaves. The women,
when the time came, started dancing.
Suddenly their wands were whirling,
then the women, whirling, spinning,
were crying out, "O Iacchus,
O Bromius, O son of Zeus,
O Lord of Cries,"
then everything, all of them,
the whole mountain, all the wild
animals, went Bacchic, too,
nothing was unmoved; the women ran,
and it all ran with them.

Agave came leaping past my hiding
place and I leaped out
to try to capture her,
but she was howling now: "Bitches,
dogs who hunt with me, it's *us*
these men are hunting! Look! Follow
me! Arm yourself with thyrsi!"
Then it was we who had to run,
to keep from being torn apart.
They swooped down on our grazing
cattle: bare-handed, they attacked.
Watch: a bellowing heifer, udders
gorged—a woman picks it bodily up,
and tears it limb from limb.
Watch now: full-grown cows,
dismembered. Ribs,
hooves, flying this way, that way,

catching on the pine boughs,
hanging there, dribbling gore.
Even bulls, all power and arrogance,
rage rising in their horns:
soft, young hands wrestle them
to the earth and flay them, faster
than your royal eyes could blink.
Then the women, like a flock of birds,
soared out across the lowlands,
along the river Asopus, where the rich
cornfields of the Thebans are.
Now, at the foot of Cithaeron,
the two hamlets, Hysiae
and Eurythrae, are invaded,
the women are attacking,
plundering. They tear children
from their houses, and whatever they put
on their backs stays there,
without straps, even bronze and iron.
They carried fire on their hair
and weren't scorched. Now the men
had had enough: in rage, they rose,
took up their weapons. What we see
next is dreadful, lord.
The men throw their spears, and draw
no blood; the women, though, let loose
their *wands*, and *wound* the men and
the men run! . . . Women defeating men!
Certainly a god was in it.
The women went back then
to the springs the god had gushed
out of the earth, and washed away
the blood, the snakes licked the drops
from their cheeks.
                    Master,
this god, whoever he may be,

I don't know, but welcome him to Thebes.
He's great in other ways as well,
but beyond all that, they say
it's he who gave mortals wine,
which eases our suffering.
If we didn't have our wine, there
wouldn't be sexual love: what pleasure
would there be for humans then?

Exit Messenger.

CHORUS LEADER

I don't know how to speak freely
to a king: I'm afraid, but I will say it,
I will cry it out: Dionysus is divine!
Dionysus cedes nothing to the other gods!

PENTHEUS

Everything is roaring closer, like a fire.
This outrage of the Bacchae:
humiliation for all Greece!
To the gates. No time to lose.
I want all the horses, all the shields;
every soldier who can snap a bowstring,
every trooper who can lift a lance.
We march on the Bacchae!
This is beyond endurance.
To have to suffer this from women!

DIONYSUS

You pretend to listen, Pentheus,
but you don't pay attention.
You wronged me, but still, I'll tell you again:
don't war against a god. Stay at peace.
Bromius won't allow his Bacchae to be driven
from where the mountain cries in ecstasy.

PENTHEUS

Don't preach at me. You were chained, you escaped.
Keep your freedom. Shall I punish you again?

DIONYSUS

In your place, I'd offer sacrifice to him,
instead of sacrilege and fighting the bit.
You're mortal, he's a god.

PENTHEUS

I'll make sacrifice. Women's blood,
pouring down the flanks of Cithaeron. As they deserve.

DIONYSUS

You'll be routed, shamed, disgraced.
They'll lift their ivied wands,
your bronze shields will wilt.

PENTHEUS

There's no way to pin this stranger, is there?
Chain him or unchain him, he still won't be quiet.

DIONYSUS

Listen, friend! We still can make this turn out well.

PENTHEUS

By doing what, obeying my own slaves?

DIONYSUS

I'll bring the women here, with no recourse to arms.

PENTHEUS

Another of your traps.

DIONYSUS

I'll use my powers to save you: is that a trap?

PENTHEUS

You and these powers conspire to save your rituals.

DIONYSUS

I have conspired, but with the god.

PENTHEUS

Bring my weapons. You: not another word.

DIONYSUS

Wait! Wouldn't you like to see them on the mountain?

PENTHEUS

See? Yes, I'd give gold to see that.

DIONYSUS

That? Why such a wild craving to see that?

PENTHEUS

I'd hate to see them drunk, if they were drunk.

DIONYSUS

Even if you hate it, though, you'd like to see?

PENTHEUS

I could hide. Under the pines, and watch quietly.

DIONYSUS

Hide or not, they might sniff you out.

PENTHEUS

Yes. Let them behold me openly.

DIONYSUS

Are you ready now? Shall I take you there?

PENTHEUS

Take me there. Let's not waste time.

DIONYSUS

First, put on a dress, a long, linen dress.

PENTHEUS

A dress? Do I have to be demoted to a woman?

DIONYSUS

If they see you as a man, they'll kill you.

PENTHEUS

You're right. Again. You always seem to know.

DIONYSUS

Dionysus taught me what to know.

PENTHEUS

What is it you know next?

DIONYSUS

We'll go inside. I'll put you in your dress.

PENTHEUS

The dress? Still? A woman's dress? Shame.

DIONYSUS

Don't you want to see the Maenads?

PENTHEUS

What sort of costume will you dress me in?

DIONYSUS

I'll put you in a wig. You'll have long curls.

PENTHEUS

Put me in a wig? . . . with long curls?

DIONYSUS

The long dress, and a net for the long curls.

PENTHEUS

Long dress . . . a net for the long curls.

DIONYSUS

Then a thyrsus for your hand; and a fawnskin.

PENTHEUS

A woman's costume? No, I won't; I can't.

DIONYSUS

Blood will flow if you battle the Bacchae.

PENTHEUS

Yes, first we have to scout them out.

DIONYSUS

Better than hunting one evil with another.

PENTHEUS

How get through the city, though, and not be seen?

DIONYSUS

We'll take the alleys and back ways: I'll lead you.

PENTHEUS

Just so the Bacchae can't mock me.
Come inside now. I'll make up my mind.

DIONYSUS

As you please, you make up your mind.

PENTHEUS

I'll go in, then either I'll come out in arms
or go with you, and follow your advice.

Exit Pentheus into the palace.

DIONYSUS

He's in the net now, women. He'll get to see
his Bacchae. He'll get what he deserves . . . to die.

Dionysus, you are near now; your task,
too, is near: your revenge, our vengeance.
Make him insane. Give him ecstasy, and madness.
In his right mind, he'd never wear that woman's dress,
but driven from his sense, he'll slide right into it.
I want him to be the laughingstock of Thebes,
led through the streets, costumed as a woman,
after all the bragging that made him seem so fearsome.
I'll go in now, I'll put him in his dress:
he'll take it to Hades with him
when his mother slaughters him.

                        Then, at last,

he'll know; Dionysus is a god.
Dionysus is the son of Zeus.
Dionysus is, for humans, fiercest and most sweet.

Exit Dionysus into the palace.

CHORUS
Oh, will I, some-
   time, in the all-
      night dances, dance
again, bare-
   foot, rapt,
      again, in
Bacchus, all
   in Bacchus,
      again?

Will I
   throw my bared
      throat
back, to the cool
   night back, the
      way,
oh, in the green joys

of the meadow, the
  way
a fawn
  frisks, leaps,
    throws itself
as it finds itself
  safely past
    the frightening
hunters, past the
  nets, the
    houndsmen
urging on
  their straining
    hounds, free
now, leaping, tasting
  free wind now,
    being wind
now as it leaps
  the plain, the
    stream
and river, out
  at last, out from
    the human,
free, back,
  into the
    green,
rich, dapple-
  shadowed tresses of the
    forest.

What is
  wisdom?
    What
the fairest
  gift the gods

can offer
us
below?
What
is nobler
than
to hold
a dominating
hand
above
the bent
head of
the enemy?
The fair, the
noble, how
we
cherish, how
we welcome
them.

Hardly
stirring, hardly
seeming
to happen, it
happens sometimes
so
slowly, the power
of the gods, but
it does, then,
stir, does
come
to pass, and,
inexorably, comes
to punish
humans,

who honor first
  self-pride, and
    turn,
their judgment
  torn, their reason
    torn,
demented, from
  the
    holy.

The first step
  of the gods, it
    hardly, in
its great
  time, seems
    to stir, the
first step
  of the godly hunt
    of
the unholy, first
  step
    of the revenge
on those who
  put themselves
    beyond
and
  over
    law.

So little
  does
    it cost
to understand
  that *this*
    has power, whatever

is divine; so
   little
     cost
to comprehend
   that what has
     long
been lawful,
   over
     centuries,
comes forever
   out
     of Nature.

What is
   wisdom?
     What
the fairest
   gift the gods
     can offer
us
   below?
     What
is nobler
   than
     to hold
a dominating
   hand
     above
the bent
   head of
     the enemy?
The fair, the
   noble, how
     we
cherish, how

we welcome
    them.

He
    is happy who,
        from the
storm, from
    the
        ocean,
reaches
    harbor, and he,
        he
is happy who,
    out of
        labor, out
of toil,
    has
        risen. And
the one
    with wealth, and
        the one with
power surpassing
    others: he
        is happy.

And hope: there
    are
        countless hopes.
Hopes
    come one
        by one, some
end well and
    others
        merely end.
But he who

lives,
>   day by
> single day,
>   in
>   happiness, he,
>   and only he,
>   will I name
>   blessed.

Enter Dionysus from the palace. He turns and calls back to Pentheus.

DIONYSUS

If you still want to see what you shouldn't see,
if you desire what shouldn't be desired, come out.
Pentheus, come out here, let me see you.
Maenad, Bacchant, woman: show us your long dress,
show us how you'll scout your mother and her troop.

Enter Pentheus, dressed as a Bacchant.

Why, you look like one of the daughters of Cadmus.
PENTHEUS
Look! What I see! I think I see two suns
and Thebes, too, twice: the seven-gated fortress, twice.
And you, you seem to be a bull, out there before me,
the double horns sprouting on your forehead:
were you an animal before, the way now you're a bull?
DIONYSUS
The god is with us now. He's not angry now.
He's made peace. You see now what you ought to see.
PENTHEUS
What do I look like now?
Do I stand like Ino or my mother?
DIONYSUS
When I see you, I might be seeing them.
Wait, a curl has come loose.
I'll tuck it in its net, it must have fallen.

PENTHEUS

It must have fallen. I was in there dancing
Bacchic dances, shaking my head backwards and forwards . . .

DIONYSUS

Hold your head still now. I'll be your maid.
I'll put the curl back, like this.

PENTHEUS

You'll put it back. Yes, I'm in your hands.

DIONYSUS

But wait, your sash has slipped. The pleats
are disarrayed; the hem is too low.

PENTHEUS

Not on the right too low; on the left, though . . .
Watch, when I lift my left leg, this way . . .

DIONYSUS

You're going to think that I'm your closest friend,
when you see how surprisingly chaste the Bacchae are.

PENTHEUS

Would a good Bacchant hold her thyrsus this way,
in her right hand, or like this, in her left?

DIONYSUS

The right hand, yes. Now the right leg, lift that.
I commend your change of mind.

PENTHEUS

Tell me, could I lift Cithaeron now—
Bacchae, cliffs, all of it: could I?

DIONYSUS

You could, if you wanted to. Your mind before
wasn't healthy, now you have the mind you should.

PENTHEUS

Will I need levers, or shall I tear the cliffs up
with my hands and put them on my shoulders?

DIONYSUS

Now wait: don't destroy the Nymphs' groves,
the sacred places where Pan plays his flute.

PENTHEUS

You're right. One shouldn't need brute force
to conquer women. I'll stay out of sight in the pines.

DIONYSUS

You'll have the proper hiding place to hide;
then, when you're hidden, you'll spy on the Maenads.

PENTHEUS

Yes, I can see them now, in the bushes,
little birds, trapped in the toils of love.

DIONYSUS

That's your mission, isn't it? To keep an eye on them?
You might catch them at it, unless they catch you . . .

PENTHEUS

Take me through Thebes now. Let all Thebes see
the single person man enough to dare all this.

DIONYSUS

You and only you will suffer for this city.
Ordeals await you, they are fated for you.
Come, I'll lead you there safely.
You'll return with someone else.

PENTHEUS

My mother . . .

DIONYSUS

. . . a model for all men . . .

PENTHEUS

That's my purpose.

DIONYSUS

You'll be carried home . . .

PENTHEUS

You're spoiling me!

DIONYSUS

. . . in your mother's arms.

PENTHEUS

. . . No, you're *spoiling* me.

DIONYSUS

Yes, I *want* to spoil you, in my way.

PENTHEUS

I'll have what I deserve.

DIONYSUS

You'll have the outcome you deserve.
You are awe-inspiring.
Your outcome will inspire awe.
Your fame will reach the heavens.

Exit Pentheus towards Cithaeron.

Agave! Listen to me! Listen to me, daughters
of Cadmus! I am calling! Hold out your hands!
I lead this young man to his ordeal.
The victory will be for me, and for Bromius.
The rest will be revealed.

Exit Dionysus.

CHORUS
Now, hounds,
  now,
    quickly, hounds
of madness, quickly
  to the mountain,
    quickly
to the bands
  of Cadmus' daughters—
    sting
them, goad
  them on,
    lead
them to the man
  costumed
    as a woman, to
the frenzied
  spy, goad
    them. First his
mother will

see him, on
    the smooth
stone cliff, or
    on his tree, will
    see him
watching, and
    will call
    the others
to her, the other
    Maenads to
    be with her.
"Who is
    this?" she'll
    call. "Who
is this who
    searches for
    the
daughters of
    Cadmus in the
    mountain,
on our
    mountain?
    Bacchae,"
she'll
    call, "*Bacchae,*
    was he
from woman
    born? *Who*
    dared
spill blood to
    bear him? Surely
    not a
woman, surely
    a
    lioness, yes,
not a

woman but some
  monstrous
Gorgon, from
  Lydia, a
    monster."

Justice
  now! Let justice
    go
forth clearly
  now! Justice
    goes
forth with
  her sword
    now!
Justice thrusts
  through
    the throat
now of the
  godless, lawless
    unjust son
of Echion, earth-
  born offspring
    of the snake.

No justice and no
  judgment and
    no
law has he, to
  rise against
    you, Bacchic
one, against your
  secret worship
    and your
mother's; with

force, insanity,
frenzy,
did he
rise as
though
to conquer the
unconquerable
with his frenzy and
his force.
Death,
though,
death will
temper him and
tame him; implacable
death chastises
minds which
do
not understand the
things
of gods.

To understand
that we
are mortal
is to live
without insufferable
pain.

I hardly envy
wisdom; my
joy,
instead, is
hunting down
those other
values, great

and clear, that
     lead
life towards
     the
          good:
to be, day-
     long, night-
          long,
reverent,
     pure, and
          to
give my
     honor to
          the gods
by casting
     out
          those customs
which
     are outside
          justice.

Justice
     now! Justice
          goes
forth clearly
     now! Justice
          goes
forth with
     her sword
          now!
Justice thrusts
     through
          the throat
now of the
     godless, lawless,

            unjust son
of Echion, earth-
    born offspring
        of the snake.

A bull be,
    Bacchus, or a
        serpent, many-
headed, be,
    or a lion,
        like a flame
be. Hunt
    the hunter,
        Bacchus, hunt
him, be the
    fighter, Bacchus, now,
        throw the net
now, laughing, lethal,
    pull him
        down now, let
him fall,
    beneath
        the herd
of Maenads, let
    him fall
        now.

Enter Messenger.

MESSENGER

O house, O famous house:
all Greece once thought you fortunate.
Cadmus came from Sidon, sowing the earth-
born dragon's harvests in the serpent's land.
Now I, a slave, mourn for you.

CHORUS

What? What news from the Bacchae?

MESSENGER

The son of Echion, Pentheus, is dead.

CHORUS

King Bromius! You
reveal your
greatness!

MESSENGER

What are you saying? What do these words mean?
Does my master's anguish give you joy?

CHORUS

Ecstasy, for
us, the Asian
strangers: no
chains, no
terror
now!

MESSENGER

Do you think no men are left in Thebes?

CHORUS

Dionysus now! Not
Thebes!
Dionysus
has power
over
me!

MESSENGER

I can pardon what you feel—still, women:
rejoicing in misfortune isn't right.

CHORUS

What doom, tell
me, did he
die,
the tyrant, the

man of unjust
accomplishments?
MESSENGER
When we'd marched out of Thebes, past
the last farms, then the river Asopus, we headed
into the hills of Cithaeron, Pentheus and I—
I was accompanying my master—and the stranger
who was the escort for our spying mission.
After a while we stopped: grass, a valley.
Stay down, be quiet, watch your step—
we want to see, not be seen. Ahead of us,
the hills move in: cliffs, a cut,
water wandering through, pines and shade,
and there they are, sitting quietly, the Maenads,
peacefully working with their hands.
A few were wreathing tendrils of ivy on a tattered
thyrsus, some were chanting Bacchic songs
to one another, like fillies when their harnesses
are taken off at night. Pentheus,
though, poor Pentheus, couldn't see the women.
"Stranger," he said, "from where we are—
I can't make them out, the impostor Maenads.
If I could climb a high pine on the cliff,
I could see their shameless orgies."

Suddenly, the stranger now: a miracle.
He reaches into the sky, and, seizing the topmost
branch of a pine tree, he drags it down,
down and down, until it touches the black earth,
until it's bent, curved, the way a bow is curved,
the way a wooden rim is curved on pegs to form a wheel.

With his two hands the stranger bent it, tough
mountain pine: this wasn't mortal's work.
Now, taking Pentheus, he puts him on the branches

of the pine and, sliding the trunk through his hands,
he lets it rise . . . gently, though, so it wouldn't
throw its rider. Pentheus wasn't thrown,
he rode it up until it towered
into the towering air, and the Maenads
saw him . . . He didn't see them, though.

Now, suddenly, as Pentheus appeared in the sky,
the stranger vanished and a voice was in the sky—
it had to have been Dionysus—crying:
"Women! I've brought the man who mocks us:
you, me, my mysteries—take revenge!"

As he cried, a light of sacred fire formed,
linking earth and heaven: the high air
suddenly went still, and everything, sky, forest,
leaf and creature, everything was still.

The women, too, not sure what they had heard,
stood still, looking around them. Then the voice
again, his command, clearer now, and they heard it
now, the daughters of Cadmus; Agave, the mother
of Pentheus, her sisters, all the Bacchae
heard him now, and understood, and ran,
flew, like darting doves, through the glade,
over the boiling stream, over the jagged stones.
They were soaring now, the god's breath maddening them.
Finally they saw him, Pentheus, in his tree.
Scaling a cliff that towered across from him,
they pitched stones at their pitiful target,
and branches, and some even threw their thyrsi.
He was out of reach of their passion,
but he was helpless, wretched, treed.
They sheared limbs from oaks then, and there they were,
with wooden levers, prying at the roots.

Again they failed. Then Agave shouted:
"Maenads, here! Circle the tree! Hold on to it!
We have to catch the animal who's mounted there.
He'll reveal the secrets of the dances of the god!"
How many hands were on that tree!
They wrenched it from the ground. And he,
he fell . . . So high he was, and he was falling,
moaning: he'd begun to understand his doom.

The first one at him was the priestess of the slaughter,
his own mother. She fell upon him, and he,
that she, poor Agave, might recognize him, tore
his headband off and, touching her cheek, shrieked
at her: "*Me!* It's me! It's Pentheus, Mother.
Your son! You are my *mother*! Look at me!
I've made mistakes, but I'm your son: don't kill me!"

Agave was foaming at the mouth, though.
Her eyes were rolling, wild; she was mad,
utterly possessed by Bacchus: what Pentheus said
was nothing to her. She took him by the arm,
the left arm, under the elbow, then she planted
a foot against his ribs and tore his arm off.
Not by herself: it was the power of the god
that put so much force into her hands.

Ino was working at his other side,
clawing at the flesh. And Autonoe
and the rest of them, the whole horde of them,
were swarming over him and everything
by then was one horrifying scream:
he, groaning with the little breath left in him,
they, howling in triumph. One had a forearm,
one had one of his feet, still warm in its sandal.
His ribs were stripped of flesh, and all the women,

all those bloody hands, were throwing pieces of him
back and forth between them as though it were a game.

Now the body is scattered. Parts at the base
of the cliff, parts hidden in the undergrowth.
His pitiful head his mother happened on;
she took it in her hands, impaled it,
like a mountain lion's, on her thyrsus,
and now she's carrying it home across Cithaeron,
leaving her sisters in the dances of the Maenads.
She's here now, in Thebes, carrying her hideous
trophy, exulting, calling on her Bacchus,
her partner in the hunt, comrade in the capture—
but all her crown of victory will really be
is tears. I want away from this calamity.
I'm leaving now, before Agave reaches the palace.
To know your human limits, to revere the gods,
is the noblest and I think the wisest course
that mortal men can follow.

Exit Messenger.

CHORUS
    Dance
        now! Exult
        and dance
    now, Bacchae!
        Exult and dance the
            misery of
    Pentheus, offspring
        of
            the Snake, who
    took a woman's
        dress, took
            the
    holy

thyrsus and
took with it the
road marked out
by the Bull, to
Hades.

O Theban
Bacchae! What
a song of
victory have you
wailed, what
triumph wailed,
a victory of tears
and
mourning. How
lovely is
the conflict, how
lovely,
with one's bloody
hand
embracing,
lovely, one's
own
child!

But here is Agave, here is the mother of Pentheus.
Her eyes are wild. Welcome now the joyous
dancers of the God of Evohe!

Enter Agave. She carries the head of Pentheus.

AGAVE
Bacchae! Asians!
CHORUS
What do you
want of
us?

AGAVE

Look what we
   have! What we
      bring home!

CHORUS

We can
   see it. I welcome you,
      fellow dancer.

AGAVE

I caught it by
   myself,
      this offspring
of a savage
   lion, and with no
      net: look!

CHORUS

In what
   wilderness?

AGAVE

      Cithaeron . . .

CHORUS

Cithaeron? . . .

AGAVE

      . . . butchered him.

CHORUS

      Who
struck him
   first?

AGAVE

      I
had the honor first.

CHORUS

   Blessed
      Agave!

AGAVE

So I'm called

among my
  pack!
            CHORUS
No
  one else? . . .
              AGAVE
    Cadmus . . .
            CHORUS
Cadmus?
              AGAVE
  His daughters,
    after me,
after I
  had touched,
    touched,
too, the
  beast. Blessed
    hunting!
Now take part
  in
    the feast!
            CHORUS
Take
  part? Pitiful
    woman!
              AGAVE
Look, though,
  the bull
    is
young, look,
  his mane
    is soft, his
cheeks
  are barely
  ' downed.

CHORUS

At least he
  seems, yes,
    with
his mane, to be
  a savage
    animal.

AGAVE

Our god, Bacchus,
  hunter,
    whipped,
cunningly, his pack
  of women on
    the beast!

CHORUS

Our lord god,
  yes, is a
    hunter.

AGAVE

Do you praise
  me?

CHORUS

  I
praise
  you.

AGAVE

  And
the Cadmeans,
  soon? . . .

CHORUS

. . . and
your son, Pentheus . . .

AGAVE

. . . will praise his
  mother for . . .

CHORUS
. . . her savage . . .

AGAVE
. . . catch, lion . . .

CHORUS
. . . born, prod-
igious . . .

AGAVE
. . . catch . . .

CHORUS
. . . caught
prodigiously.

AGAVE
Prodigious
catch.

CHORUS
Do you
exult?

AGAVE
I
exult!
Greatness have
I
accomplished, great
the deeds, great
and shining!

CHORUS LEADER
Show it now, poor woman. Show your blessed trophy
to the people. Let them behold your victory.

AGAVE
Thebans! Citizens!
Everyone who lives beneath these high towers,
look! Come see the beast the daughters of Cadmus
hunted down, not with nets, not with spears,
but with the white nails of our hands.
Who is the hunter, armed with useless spears,

who'll dare boast now, when all we needed
were our hands to bring the creature down
and tear it completely to pieces?

Where's my father?
Old, good Cadmus, he should be here.
And my child, Pentheus, find him for me, too.
Have him bring a ladder; have him stand it
here to nail the lion's head to the cornice.
I captured it myself, and brought it here.

Enter Cadmus, with attendants carrying a litter
with the remains of Pentheus.

CADMUS

Come this way, please . . . Put the dreadful burden
which was Pentheus here, before the palace.
I've brought the body back: I searched forever.
It was in the folds of Cithaeron, torn to shreds,
scattered through the impenetrable forest,
no two parts of him in any single spot.
When they described the atrocity my daughters
had committed, I'd returned to the walls of the town
with old Tiresias: we'd been with the Bacchae.
I turned back again, up to the mountain,
where I gathered the body of this boy,
murdered by the Maenads. I saw Autonoe there,
Aristaeus' wife, the mother of poor Actaeon,
and I saw Ino, both of them, still in the thickets,
pitiful women, still stung with frenzy, still insane.
Now someone has told me that Agave,
still possessed by the god, has come to Thebes . . .
And they were right, I see her,
a dismal sight to have to behold.

AGAVE

Father, you can boast now; the daughters you sired
are more noble than any other mortal's.
I speak of all of us, but especially me,

who have left the loom and shuttle and risen
to greatness: hunting wild creatures with my hands.

Look what I have here in my arms:
a trophy for the palace. Here, Father,
take it in your hands, glory in my kill.
Invite your friends to feast, for you
are blessed, blessed by our accomplishments.

CADMUS

I cannot watch this. This is grief that has no measure.
What your poor hands accomplished was butchery.
A lovely victim you have murdered for the gods,
whom you call for Thebes and me to celebrate.
Anguish for you, anguish, too, for me.
With justice, but with too much severity,
Lord Bromius, our own blood, has ruined us.

AGAVE

Complaining, scowling: old age makes men sour!
Would my son at least could be a happy hunter,
like his mother, when he goes out on the chase
with his young friends from Thebes.
But all he does is struggle with the god.
Father, he needs talking to, by you.
Someone call him, let me see him.
Let him see his mother, Agave the blessed.

CADMUS

Child, if consciousness should come to you
of what you've done, how grievously you'll suffer.
If you could pass your life in your present mind,
we'd never call you happy but at least
you wouldn't know how miserable you are.

AGAVE

But this is wonderful! What could cause pain here?

CADMUS

First, turn your eyes upwards, towards the sky.

AGAVE

There. Why should I look into the sky, though?

CADMUS

Does the sky look the same? Might it be changing?

AGAVE

Yes, it is; it's more transparent, clearer.

CADMUS

And do you still feel flurries of excitement in you?

AGAVE

I don't know what you mean . . . No . . . Yes . . .
Yes, something is changing, my mind is calmer.

CADMUS

Can you hear me? Can you answer clearly?

AGAVE

What were we saying, Father? I've forgotten.

CADMUS

In whose household did you marry?

AGAVE

You gave me to Echion, the sown-man they called him.

CADMUS

And what child did you bear your husband there?

AGAVE

Pentheus was the outcome of our marriage.

CADMUS

Now, whose head are you holding in your arms?

AGAVE

A lion's . . . The huntresses . . . They told me . . .

CADMUS

Look right at it. One look will be enough.

AGAVE

What? What am I seeing? What is in my hands?

CADMUS

Look carefully. Study it more closely.

AGAVE

I see horror. I see suffering. I see grief.

CADMUS

Does it still look like a lion?

AGAVE

No, Pentheus: I am holding his head.

CADMUS

Yes, now you know, I mourn Pentheus.

AGAVE

Who killed him? Why is he in *my* hands?

CADMUS

Savage truth, how long you took to come to light.

AGAVE

Tell me, my heart is trembling with it.

CADMUS

You killed him. With your sisters.

AGAVE

Where did it happen? At home? Where?

CADMUS

Where Actaeon was dismembered by his hounds.

AGAVE

On Cithaeron? Why was my poor Pentheus there?

CADMUS

He went to mock the gods, and your rituals.

AGAVE

But we, why were we there?

CADMUS

You were mad. The city was possessed by Dionysus.

AGAVE

I see now. Dionysus has destroyed us.

CADMUS

You enraged him. You denied he was god.

AGAVE

My son's beloved body, where is it, Father?

CADMUS

There he is, what I could find of him.

AGAVE

Is he decently put back together?

Why did Pentheus have to suffer for my madness?

CADMUS

He, too, refused the god, and the god,
for this, has ruined us all—
you, this boy: our whole house is ruined.
And I, with no male heirs, have to see him now,
this branching of your womb, the new light
of our house, shamefully destroyed.

O child, you held our house together, you,
my daughter's son, how the city was in awe of you.
No one looking at your face would dare affront my age—
you'd have punished them as they deserved.
Now I'll be exiled, my honors stripped from me.
I, the great Cadmus, sower of the race of Thebes,
who harvested the most lovely of harvests.
O dearest of men, you are no longer living
but you are still, child, among those I love
beyond all else. Who will stroke my beard now?
Who embrace me, call me Grandfather, ask me,
"Has anyone offended you, old man, not shown you
adequate respect? Disturbed, dishonored you?
Tell me who it was, Grandfather, I'll punish him."
Now I am nothing. You, a ruin. Your mother
only to be pitied, and her unhappy sisters, too.
Is there anyone who scorns the gods? Look now
at this murdered boy: now, believe!

CHORUS LEADER

I grieve with you, Cadmus: your daughter's son
has justice now, but so much grief for you.

AGAVE

Father, look at me, how my destiny has turned.

She kneels to the body of Pentheus.

Who is this person? Who is this corpse?
Who am I? How can I, in all reverence,

knowing that my hands dismembered him
and are polluted with his blood,
dare to touch him, dare take him
to my breast, dare sing his dirge to him?
But how can I not? What other hands
can care for you, my child?

O old man, come help me, help me
touch this wretched boy. Show me
where to lay his head, show me how
to put his body back together.

Look, his arms are so well muscled,
his legs so strong, but his face, oh,
dearest face, its cheek is barely feathered.
This flesh I nurtured once, I kiss.
The fragments of this body I loved
once, I lay in place.

How am I doing this? How can I touch
my crime with my polluted hands?
With what robes shall I veil you, child?
Here: I'll give you mine. I'll hide your head.
Here, hide your shattered, bloodstained body.

She covers the body with her veil.
Dionysus appears, as himself, above.

DIONYSUS

I am Dionysus. I am Bacchus.
Bromius and Iacchus.
Dithyrambus and Evius.
I am the son of Zeus.
I have come to the country of the Thebans,
where Semele, the daughter of King Cadmus,
bore me in a blaze of lightning.

When I arrived in Thebes, there was blasphemy.
"He was born of mortals," they were saying.
Slander. Irreverence. Impiety.
I offered these people everything.
How did they repay my generosity?
With malice, ingratitude, and lies.

Now I shall recite your future for you.
First, your future will be suffering.
Then your future will be suffering again.
Banishment and slavery and pain.
You will be driven from this city.
You will be hounded into other lands.
Captives in a war.
Chains. Slavery. Toil.
Your lives will wear away like sand.

Behold our Pentheus. He found the death
he deserved: torn to pieces.

You beheld him. You beheld his lies.
His impudence. You beheld him
when he tried to chain me and abused me
and tried—and *dared* to try—
to punish me.
I am Dionysus! Behold me!

The hands that should have been the last
to do this to him were the very hands
that did it. Why? Because he did
what he should not have done.

And now your doom, Agave, is this:
for you and for your sisters—exile.
You must expiate your crime.

You are polluted, you cannot stay
in the precincts of these graves.

And Cadmus: there are ordeals for you.
You will be transfigured into a snake.
And Harmonia, the daughter of Ares, whom you won
as wife despite your being mortal,
she, too, will be a beast, a snake.
Then both of you, drawn by oxen in a cart,
will, according to the oracle of Zeus,
lead an innumerable barbarian horde
to lay waste cities, to ravage and destroy.
And when the shrine of Apollo is sacked,
the hordes will turn, and the turning,
and the coming back, will be tragic.

Ares, in the end, will save you and save
Harmonia and bring your lives
into the country of the blessed.

This is the decree of Dionysus,
the son not of a human but of Zeus.
If you had understood your mortal natures
when you refused to understand them,
the son of Zeus would have been your ally.
You would now be in blessedness.

CADMUS

Dionysus, we implore you, we have offended.

DIONYSUS

You learned too late to know me.
When you had time, you did not know me.

CADMUS

We confess that, but your punishment is harsh.

DIONYSUS

I am a god! You outraged my divinity.

CADMUS

Gods should not resemble mortals in anger.

DIONYSUS

Long ago, my father, Zeus, ordained all this.

AGAVE

Father, the sentence is decreed: banishment.

DIONYSUS

Why do you delay your doom?

CADMUS

Oh, my child, to what a terrible fate
have we been reduced.
You, your pitiful sisters, and myself, all wretched.
An old man, to have to live a stranger among strangers.
There is an oracle as well that I will lead
a ragged barbarian army against Hellas. My wife,
Harmonia, the daughter of Ares, will be a savage snake,
and I, too, will be a snake, and against the altars
and the graves of Greece will lead those spears.
And no respite. I will cross the river Acheron,
as it plunges down, and have, still, no peace.

AGAVE

And me, O Father, banishment!
To be torn from you!

CADMUS

My poor child, why put your arms around me?
A white swan sheltering its hoary, helpless father.

AGAVE

Tell me, where shall I go, outcast from my country?

CADMUS

I don't know, child. Your father is no help.

AGAVE

Farewell, my house; farewell,
my country. Banished from my home,
exiled from everything I love.
What is left for me?

CADMUS

Poor daughter: go to Aristaeus, Actaeon's father.

AGAVE

I am mourning for you, Father.

CADMUS

And I, daughter, these tears are for you,
and for your sisters.

AGAVE

How terrible the blows Dionysus
struck against your house.

DIONYSUS

I suffered terribly,
my name, in Thebes, deprived of honor.

AGAVE

Goodbye, Father.

CADMUS

Child, poor child, farewell.
Faring well, though, will be hard for you.

AGAVE

Take me away from here, to my sisters,
the sisters of my endless exile.
Let awful Cithaeron never see me again.
Let me never set my eyes on Cithaeron again,
and let me never see another thyrsus,
to bring this back to me again.

All of that I leave, all
of it, to other Bacchae.

Exit Agave.

CHORUS

Many forms are
there of the
divine.
Many things the

gods accomplish
  unexpectedly.
What we waited
  for does not
    come to pass, while
for what remained
  undreamed the god
    finds ways.
Just such
  doing was this
    doing.

Exit all.

CPSIA information can be obtained
at www.ICGtesting.com
Printed in the USA
LVHW03s1955200618
581391LV00001B/73/P